PENNY BLUE

PENNY BLUE

PENNY BLUE

by Vanessa Brooks

WARNER CHAPPELL PLAYS

LONDON

A Time Warner Company

PENNY BLUE
First published in 1994
by Warner Chappell Plays Ltd
129 Park Street, London W1Y 3FA

Copyright © 1994 by Vanessa Brooks

The author asserts her moral right to be identified as the author of the work.

ISBN 0 85676 199 0

For Jack and Velma Paterson,
Christopher Rickwood
and with thanks to Alan Ayckbourn

PENNY BLUE was first presented at the Stephen Joseph Theatre, Scarborough on 22nd June, 1994, with the following cast:

BOB	Adrian McLoughlin
MARION	Maggie Wells
PEN	Cathy Sara
DOUGIE	Stephen Hattersley
PETULA	Jill Benedict
TREVOR	Damien Goodwin

Directed by Malcolm Hebden
Designed by Jan Bee Brown
Lighting Design by Jackie Staines

CHARACTERS

BOB   Forties. Car mechanic.

MARION   Forties. Part-time barmaid.

PEN   Sixteen. Their daughter. Unemployed.

DOUGIE   Forties. Self-made man. Naturalised
                        Australian.

PETULA   Forties. Naturalised Australian.

TREVOR   Twenties. Unemployed.

The action takes place in BOB and MARION'S flat on the
fourteenth floor of a tower block on the edge of the East End
of London.

ACT ONE: An October evening.

ACT TWO: The following afternoon.

ACT ONE

The living room. Two exits, one leading into hallway and bedrooms, the other into kitchen. A balcony on two sides.

BOB, on hands and knees, unscrews the cover from the hot air ventilation system on the wall. He looks into the hole holding a shoe above his head.

MARION   (*off*) Bob. Bob. Bob!

BOB   Come on. Come on, you little devils. Show yourselves. Out you come. Daddy's waiting.

     (MARION *appears in the hallway exit dragging a Z-bed.*)

MARION   Bob.

BOB   Ssssh.

MARION   Do you think Australians like potato waffles?

     (BOB *suddenly beats at something frantically with his shoe.*)

BOB   Yes! Yes! Yes! Yes! Gotcha. Come here. Die! Die you little . . .

MARION   What on earth do you think you're doing? They're due here any minute and you've got your head stuck up that bloody hole again.

BOB   Damn it.

MARION   Not as if you ever catch any.

BOB   Must have heard you.

MARION   Don't be silly. Cockroaches don't have ears.

BOB   Pick up vibrations, don't they? Through their wobbly wotsits.

MARION   Antennae.

BOB   That's the ticket. Blow it.

MARION   Will you please put that grill back on. You can
            help me with this if you're at a loose end.

            (MARION *makes up the Z-bed behind the sofa.* BOB
            remains preoccupied with the ventilation system.)

BOB   They eat kiwi fruit and mangoes.

MARION   I'd like to know where madam's got to. It's late
            opening Fridays. She should've sailed through
            the checkout.

BOB   Except when they're in the Bush. Then it's
            berries. And worms that live in trees.

MARION   What?

BOB   Lots of meat too, of course. Big meat eaters.

MARION   Cockroaches?

BOB   Australians.

MARION   Did you go to the Off-License?

BOB   Anyway they're not Australians. Londoners.
            Same as us. Moved location that's all. I mean if
            we upped sticks and moved to the South of France
            what would that make us?

MARION   Rich.

BOB   What I'm saying is you can't change what you
            are can you. Eh? It's blood. It's roots. It's in your
            bones. Go anywhere in the world and you're still
            English.

MARION   Jeremy Paxman says we're Europeans now.

BOB   Eh?

MARION   Interviewed him in his conservatory. I read it.
            Croissant for breakfast. Sauerkraut for tea. A

cellar full of German lager because it doesn't
make you burp as much as the English variety.

BOB   Where do you read this rubbish?

MARION   Dougie and Petula are naturalised now anyway.
             They've got passports and everything.

BOB   So?

MARION   So they are now Australian. Full stop. I asked you
             a question.

BOB   I'll pop out later.

MARION   Bob. We've got two tins of tango and half a bottle
             of eggnog with a skin on top.

BOB   Should have told Pen-Pen to stock up at the
             supermarket.

MARION   She's sixteen. It's illegal.

BOB   Huh. Don't think that'd stop her.

MARION   Don't start creating. Not today. My ears are still
             hurting from last night's slanging match.

BOB   Wearing those boots again. Doctor Martens. I ask
             you.

MARION   It's fashionable. Wore some funny things yourself
             when you were sixteen.

BOB   I always looked presentable.

MARION   Selective memory, that's what you've got.
             Drainpipe trousers and bumfreezer jacket.

BOB   Didn't hear you complaining.

             (MARION *picks up tin of polish and duster and
             starts to work.*)

MARION   Enough grease on your hair to cook a pan full of
           sausages. That was before you started on the
           eighteen inch flares and that Afghan coat that
           smelled of mouldy cheese.

BOB   In our day girls looked like girls. She looks like a
           navvie. Manners the same too.

MARION   She's at a difficult age.

BOB   So am I.

MARION   Don't I know it.

BOB   So its all my fault, is it?

MARION   Will you put that bloody grill back on! Going to
           have to hoover again, aren't I?

BOB   I'll do it with the sweeper.

           (BOB *screws grill back in place.*)

MARION   I don't want any of your displays in front of
           Dougie and Petula. Do you hear me?

BOB   I thought tomorrow we could amble up to the
           Three Feathers. Like the old days. Sink a few
           pints. Make up doubles. Shoot some pool.

MARION   Promise me.

BOB   For God's sake Marion!

MARION   Bob.

BOB   If she towed the line and buckled-to we wouldn't
           have all this palaver every other minute!

MARION   Bob.

BOB   Not me who walks around with a face like a
           tombstone snapping my head off whenever I'm
           spoken to.

MARION   Bob.

BOB	And now she's hankering after some ferry trip across the channel. I ask you. Give. Give. Give. All I bloody do.
MARION	Bob!
BOB	What?
MARION	Have a bit of patience. Different world these days. Life's not as simple as it was when we were kids.
BOB	You're telling me. If I'd given the lip to my parents that she gives us I'd have been booted into the middle of next week.
MARION	You did. And you were. And look at the good it's done you. Finished?
BOB	Where's the sweeper?
MARION	In the hall cupboard.

(BOB *exits.* MARION *dusts the display cabinet.*)

MARION	Where it's been for the past fourteen years.

(BOB *enters with carpet sweeper. He watches* MARION *with interest.*)

BOB	Love.
MARION	Yes.
BOB	Just. Well. Just nudge those trophies to the front, eh? So we can see them better.
MARION	Oh honestly.
BOB	Dougie'll be interested. Always fancied himself a sportsman.
MARION	I hate to burst your bubble Bob, but you bought this trophy yourself because you thought you'd been cheated out of the darts tournament.

BOB   I was cheated.

           (MARION *takes another trophy out of the cabinet.*)

MARION   And the snooker.

BOB   Yes.

           (MARION *picks up another trophy.*)

MARION   Even the Trivial Pursuit. There wasn't even a cup
           going for that but you went and bought yourself
           one anyway.

BOB   He's not to know. Got to keep my end up.

           (BOB *sweeps carpet around grill.*)

MARION   I hope you're planning on changing before they
           arrive.

BOB   Eh?

MARION   Been wearing those trousers since yesterday.

BOB   So? I haven't been rolling around in the mud.

MARION   You've had your head up the ventilation shaft
           haven't you?

BOB   Yeah. My head. Not my . . .

MARION   Just do it Bob. Please. For me. Put your nice
           beige slacks on. They're in the airing cupboard.
           Shave wouldn't kill you either.

BOB   What do you think they'll be like?

MARION   Cheese straws.

BOB   What?

           (MARION *dashes out to kitchen.*)

BOB   Must have been what . . . '77 when they left.
              Here. Here — Marion! Remember Dougie's party
              trick?

              (MARION *enters holding a cheese straw in an oven
              glove.*)

MARION   Taste.

              (MARION *puts cheese straw into* BOB'S *mouth.*)

BOB   Oooh. Hot. You know. He'd pretend to eat a
              cigarette. A lit cigarette. Then he'd pop it out of
              his mouth and it'd still be burning.

MARION   It wasn't funny then. Well?

BOB   Um. Nice. Cheesy.

              (MARION *dashes out again.*)

BOB   And Petula. What a corker she was. First time I
              saw her she was hanging around for Dougie
              outside Aldgate tube eating a bag of chips and
              sucking on a saveloy.

              (MARION *enters with* BOB'S *electric shaver. She
              turns it on and puts it in* BOB'S *hand and places it
              on his cheek. He shaves.* MARION *takes glasses
              from display cabinet and polishes them with a
              cloth.*)

BOB   Standing there smelling of vinegar with chip
              grease on her chin. In that skirt. The mini skirt.
              You know. The one with the tassels and her red
              plastic boots. Dead ringer for Marianne Faithful.

MARION   With National Health glasses and buck teeth.

BOB   I tell you. If you hadn't been the love of my
              life . . .

MARION   Ha.

BOB   Could've been me instead of Dougie.

MARION   Doubt it. You didn't have Dougie's wallet.
            Always one for the highlife, Petula.

            (MARION *spots* BOB *about to light a cigarette.*)

MARION   No you don't.

BOB   What? What are you doing. Oi!

MARION   Not in here please. If you must light up. On the
            balcony.

BOB   Are you telling me I've got to stand out there in
            the cold every time I have a fag?

MARION   Just for now. I've got everything smelling nice.

BOB   Bloody reformed smokers. Self righteous. That's
            what you are. Given up the fags, gained a
            sainthood.

MARION   Wouldn't do you any harm. You should hear
            yourself in the night. Its like sleeping next to a
            faulty vacuum cleaner. Shoes by the front door,
            thank you.

            (MARION *picks up* BOB'S *shoes from beside the
            ventilation grill and exits.* BOB *leans over the
            balcony and looks down at the communal gardens
            below.*)

BOB   Would you believe it? Vandals. Up to their tricks
            again. Only put those saplings in two days ago
            and already half of them are missing their
            branches. Razor wire did a fat lot of good. What's
            to gain, eh? Oh. Hello. Oh yes. Here we go.

            (MARION *returns. She lifts rug to discover
            newspaper and crisp wrappers beneath.*)

MARION   Can't anyone use a bin around here?

            (MARION *picks up rubbish and exits.*)

BOB   A bloody great German shepherd and that woman
           with the neck brace and her three spaniels.

           (MARION *enters, picks up rug and shakes it over
           the balcony.*)

BOB   Signs everywhere. Even those machines that sell
           whatsits.

MARION   Pooperscoopers.

BOB   Pooperscoopers. Do they take a blind bit of notice
           . . . makes my blood boil. Blatant too. Look. Bold
           as brass.

MARION   Don't start, Bob. There's nothing you can do.

BOB   Look at that idiot!

MARION   Which idiot?

BOB   Him. Him. That great gangly streak of lightning.
           Where the turf's been dug up. With the pit bull
           terrier. Just letting it . . .

MARION   Come inside. No scenes please.

BOB   OI! OI — YOU!

MARION   Bob! Stop it!

BOB   MY GARDEN TOO, MATE! COMMUNAL!
           THAT'S MINE, TOO! WHAT DO YOU THINK
           IT IS — A DOG'S TOILET?

MARION   Honestly.

BOB   He's making out he can't hear me. YES! YOU!
           BEANPOLE!

           (MARION *grabs* BOB *and drags him inside.*)

MARION   What are you playing at?

BOB   What?

MARION   Go and change your trousers!

BOB   Don't talk to me like I'm a little boy.

MARION   Stop behaving like one! You know the way things
            are around here at the moment. You don't want
            to draw attention to yourself like that.
            Repercussions. There's always repercussions.
            And I'm the one who'll end up getting mugged in
            the launderette because of your dog dirt
            obsession.

BOB   That's my garden.

MARION   No. No Bob, it isn't. A patch the size of a
            handkerchief is your garden. If you're that fond
            of it why not dig it up and keep it on the balcony.
            Maybe then we'd have some peace!

BOB   Those types don't frighten me. You've got to
            stand up to them.

MARION   All mouth no trousers!

BOB   I'm changing. I'm changing.

            (BOB *exits.* MARION *fusses. She looks at the
            eggnog bottle. Pours herself a glass with her
            back to the hallway exit.* PEN *enters, carrying two
            plastic shopping bags.*)

PEN   Are you a secret drinker?

MARION   Oh my God! Pen-Pen. Don't creep up like that.

PEN   I saw a programme. There are thousands of
            housewives all over the country who turn to the
            bottle.

MARION   Your father's been doing his amateur park keeper
            bit. My nerves are jangled. Where have you been?

PEN   Nowhere.

MARION   Nowhere must have been fascinating. You've
            been there over an hour. Success?

PEN   S'pose.

MARION   Ham and pineapple coleslaw. Often run out of
           that early. Popular line.

PEN   Yes.

MARION   Pizza slices.

PEN   Five pizza slices for the price of four. Special
           offer. Tomato ketchup. Farmhouse cheddar.
           Rindless bacon . . .

MARION   Alright. Alright. Bags in kitchen.

           (PEN *heads for kitchen.* MARION *intercepts and
           rifles through bags.*)

PEN   Bread. Mushrooms — the flat ones. Lincolnshire
           pork sausages. Two onions and a really
           disgusting white sauce mix.

MARION   Might as well dish these up now.

           (MARION *takes packets of crisps out of carrier
           bag. Moves to sideboard.*)

PEN   Four pound bag crinkle cut chips. Pasta quills
           and a tube of cream for Dad's little . . .

MARION   Kitchen.

           (PEN *exits.* MARION *finds a round partitioned
           tupperware serving tray — a 'Party Susan'.*)

MARION   What the . . . honestly Pen-Pen. Sometimes I
           think the hospital got the babies mixed up when I
           had you.

           (PEN *enters eating cheese straws.*)

PEN   Why? Because I'm too stunningly brilliant and
           amazing to be a daughter of yours?

MARION   Because you have such appalling taste.

(PEN *lies down on the Z-bed.*)

MARION   Scampi and lemon puffs. Steak and onion triangles. Oriental crab corn squares?

PEN   How long are the kangaroos staying anyway?

MARION   Lord knows what they taste like. The smell's enough to descale the kettle.

PEN   Where's Dad? I hope they're paying rent. They've made me homeless.

MARION   Tonight. They're staying the one night. Tomorrow they're going on to Stratford. Your father's changing.

PEN   Stratford. What do they want to go to Stratford for? Nothing there apart from housing estates and chip shops.

MARION   Stratford-Upon-Avon. Home of the Bard. Shakespeare and all that. They're seeing a play.

PEN   A play. What do they want to see a play for?

MARION   I don't know. I suppose it's a history lesson. If nothing else.

PEN   Boredom city. Give me the telly any day.

MARION   Will you get off that bed. You're runkling it all up. Fill up the Party Susan. Plates. I'll do the plates.

PEN   The Party what?

(PEN *crosses to table.* MARION *folds paper napkins and puts them between plates.* PEN *puts crisps into 'Party Susan'.*)

MARION   And you can stop referring to them as kangaroos. Their names are Dougie and Petula, thank you.

PEN Looks like a plastic dish to me.

MARION Very old friends. Used to do everything together. Nearly had a double wedding but your Dad and me. Not enough for frills. Bob was Dougie's best man. And I was bridesmaid. Head bridesmaid. I wore this maxi dress with silk daisies on the front. Quite a do. At the Hawksmoor church round the corner. Petula had to have a church of course. Nearly bankrupted her poor old Dad. She spent three days sobbing into her dinner before he stumped up for the honeymoon. Clever that way, Petula.

PEN Why is it called a Party Susan?

MARION And being asked to sleep on the Z-bed for a night does not constitute homelessness so you can stop pulling that one.

PEN It's a tupperware thing isn't it?

MARION I've had a word with your father. A repeat performance of yesterday's shenanigans and you won't see me for dust. All I'm asking is that you be nice to each other while the Australians are here.

PEN The fifties wasn't it? When it was big I mean. All those women in skirts like umbrellas selling plastic boxes to each other.

MARION Where's my change?

PEN I gave it all to charity. I thought that's what you'd want.

MARION Watch your cheek.

PEN I can't. My eyes are in the wrong position.

MARION Pen-Pen! Come on. I've yet to put my face on.

(PEN *digs into her pocket and hands* MARION *some coins.*)

MARION	Less of the little orphan Annies please. Have to smarten your ideas up if you want to go on that trip.
PEN	You've spoken to Dad.
MARION	You should think about going on one of those schemes.
PEN	I don't want to sweep floors and chop vegetables for twenty-odd quid a week.
MARION	I don't want to stand behind a bar all night listening to drunks but someone's got to pay for the extras. Now then. Scheme would do you good. Give you some pocket money. Could end up going somewhere.
PEN	Like Kelly?
MARION	That's different. She was always over-sensitive. All got too much for her, poor kid.
PEN	She worked six months at that leather factory. They said there'd be a job at the end of it. Police found a pile of waistcoats next to her body. She thought they'd have her back if she worked on her own time.

(BOB *enters wearing beige trousers and preposterously tight polo-neck jumper.*)

BOB	(*to* PEN) I thought you'd run away to join the circus. What do you think Marion? Sporty yet casual.

(PEN *helps herself to crisps.*)

MARION	Where did you find that jumper?
BOB	Bottom of the wardrobe. Next to the convector heater. In the black bag.
MARION	(*to* PEN) Stop eating those crisps. Bob. Honestly.

BOB   It's not dirty. Does it smell?

MARION   That bag was for the Sue Ryder lady. I'm sorry
             love but it doesn't really fit any more, does it.

BOB   It'll stretch. I thought I looked a bit like a golf
             pro.

PEN   You look like Jimmy Tarbuck on a cream
             doughnut diet.

BOB   Is she going to wear a dress?

MARION   Pen-Pen hasn't changed yet. I'm sure she'll
             surprise us.

BOB   That's what I'm afraid of.

PEN   I am here you know. I'm not getting changed.

MARION }   Yes you are.
BOB   }   Yes you are.

PEN   No I'm not.

BOB   You will do what you . . .

MARION   Go and get your things, Pen-Pen. What you need
             for the next day or so. Put them behind the sofa.

PEN   Fine.

BOB   And cover yourself up. You look like a trollop.

PEN   Love you too, Dad.

             (PEN *exits*.)

MARION   Are you starting Bob? Because if you're starting
             I'm going.

BOB   I put her mattress behind the wardrobe.

MARION   Oh Lord! The blow up.

BOB   I'll do it. You go and get ready.

MARION   By the Z-bed. Pump's there too. I'll see if I can
           crowbar her majesty into a dress.

           (MARION *exits.* BOB *sings 'Tie Me Kangaroo Down
           Sport' to himself and dances over to the deflated
           air mattress. Affixes pump, changes his mind and
           opts for blowing it up by mouth.* PEN *enters in
           dress with Doctor Martens boots. She puts her
           belongings behind sofa — a few odds and ends
           and a rucksack full of clothes. She sits and
           applies make-up from box with small mirror.*)

BOB   Do you have to do that in here? Your mother
           spent the best part of an hour last week scrubbing
           lipstick off the draylon.

PEN   She's taken over the bathroom There's an
           exclusion zone. Why don't you use the pump.
           You look even more purple than usual.

BOB   Isn't working properly. What do you mean
           purple?

           (BOB *coughs nastily.*)

PEN   You ought to be careful. You're cruising for a
           heart attack.

BOB   Are you going to put some decent shoes on?

PEN   No. I'm not.

BOB   Why don't you borrow some from your mother?

PEN   Borrow one of her A-line skirts and a middle-
           aged handbag shall I?

BOB   Talk yourself out of that day trip if you're not
           careful.

PEN   I can go then?

BOB   We'll see. This little shindig's going to set us back a few bob. Not that I begrudge it. Oh no. Can't believe it. See Dougie again. Good old Dougie. Shared a flat in our bachelor days. Lived on baked beans and milk stout. Me and Dougie were like that.

PEN   Were Mum and Petula like that too?

BOB   'Course they were. Made up a foursome. Known in all the pubs in the Whitechapel road. Used to call us the four stooges because we . . . oh never mind.

PEN   Only I got the impression Mum doesn't like Petula much. Thinks she's a money grabber.

BOB   Stop stirring Pen-Pen. We were as close as four people could be who hadn't shared the same nappies. They stayed with your mother's aunt when they first got to Australia.

PEN   Aunty Ruby.

BOB   You never met her of course. Emigrated before you were born. Practically brought your mum up. Had her own dry cleaning business just outside Sydney. Tough old bird. Kept spiders as pets. Died last year of course.

PEN   Choked on a swordfish steak.

BOB   Trust you to remember that.

PEN   Mum was really upset. That she didn't see her before she died.

BOB   Too expensive. Would've cost a grand all told. They make you look like you work on a building site. Don't show us up Pen-Pen. While they're here. Stop being clever. Be a good girl.

PEN   I don't get it.

BOB   What?

PEN   You were all great mates.

BOB   Bosom buddies.

PEN   And Dougie wasn't short of money.

BOB   Can say that again. Walk out of the flat with a
           tanner come back ten minutes later with his
           pockets full of ten bob notes.

PEN   Why did they go to Australia then?

BOB   What?

PEN   Why did they go to Australia if everything was so
           hunky dory here?

BOB   It was a good idea. At the time.

PEN   Why?

BOB   It. Just. It doesn't matter Pen.

           (MARION *enters, changed and made-up.*)

MARION   Well?

BOB   You look lovely, love.

MARION   My hair? Not too bouffant? Don't look like I've
           had an electric shock?

BOB   Smashing. You look smashing, love.

MARION   I suppose Petula will be in all her finery.
           Dripping jewellery no doubt. Bob. You'll make
           yourself ill doing that. Where's the pump? Don't
           want you having a heart attack. At that sort of age.

PEN   See.

BOB   Why do you all think I'm going to have a heart
           attack? Is it wishful thinking or something? Have
           a word about the boots Marion.

MARION   I thought tonight we could have nibbly stuff.
Pizza slices. Snacky sort of things. Proper meal
tomorrow. Give me that.

> (MARION *takes the foot pump and affixes it to
> mattress. It works perfectly.*)

BOB   You'll let the air out.

PEN   Can I put the telly on?

BOB }   No.
MARION }   No.

PEN   So I've just got to sit here in silence.

BOB }   Yes.
MARION }   Yes — put the glasses back in the cabinet, Bob.

> (BOB *does so.* MARION *pumps urgently.*)

PEN   Alright to breathe is it?

BOB   You watch television all week. Have a night off.
Learn a bit about the art of conversation.

PEN   From you?

BOB   Lip. Less of it.

PEN   Not going to learn much about the art of
conversation then am I?

MARION   Doesn't Pen-Pen look nice, Bob? She changed for
you.

PEN   I did not. I changed for me.

BOB   Why does she have to wear those bloody awful
boots?

MARION   She'll take them off in a minute.

PEN   Oh will I?

BOB   Could murder a pint. Oh. Oh.

MARION	What?
BOB	Haven't got time now.
MARION	Oh Bob. What are we going to do? They can hardly drink tap water.
PEN	I'll go.
MARION	No you won't.
BOB	We've got to be here when they arrive. It's over an hour since they called from Heathrow.

(BOB *delves into his pocket and hands* PEN *some notes.*)

MARION	It's against the law. Suppose the police walk into the shop?
BOB	The last thing the police are worried about around here is under-age drinking.
PEN	What do you want?
MARION	Take the trolley. I don't want anyone seeing you walking along with a brewery in your hands.
BOB	Case of lager. Whatever's cheap. Marion?
MARION	Gin I suppose. And mixer. Tonic water. Large bottle.
PEN	See you.
MARION	And don't get lost in nowhere land this time. Come straight back.

(PEN *exits.* MARION *hands the pumped up mattress to* BOB.)

MARION	Take it next door. I'll do the bedding later.

(BOB *exits.* MARION *smooths down the cushions. Walks onto the balcony.* BOB *enters.*)

BOB Well. All set. Won't be long now. You alright love?

(BOB *joins* MARION *on the balcony.*)

MARION Do you remember — when we saw them off from the airport?

BOB Don't I just. Only made it with a hair's breadth to spare. Silver jubilee. Street parties playing havoc with the one-way system.

MARION I was very upset.

BOB Pregnant, weren't you? Had the hormones of a stampeding elephant.

MARION Bob!

BOB You know what I mean.

MARION I was angry too. Flying to the other side of the world. Not a thought for anyone. I thought. What gives you the right to just take off. Leaving chaos behind.

BOB Love. We agreed. Bygones, eh? All forgotten.

MARION I haven't forgotten. Haven't forgotten bailing you out of Bow Street police station while they were whooping it up in the mile high club.

BOB Eh, eh, eh. We don't mention it. Concentrate on the good times.

MARION My lips are sealed. It's you I'm worried about. Go steady on the booze Bob. Promise me.

BOB Gi's a kiss.

MARION Stop it.

(BOB *pulls* MARION *towards him. Sudden bleeping of the electronic entry system.*)

MARION   Oh my God! Oh my God!

(MARION *dashes around the room checking all is in order.*)

BOB   No need to panic.

MARION   They're here. This is it.

BOB   Get the buzzer then, Marion.

(MARION *exits.* BOB *checks his trophies again. He practises holding in his stomach.* MARION *enters.*)

MARION   I buzzed the door open and watched them go into the lift. Petula's got something funny on her head.

BOB   Can't trust the video entry. Makes everyone look like Marty Feldman.

MARION   Look at the mess Pen-Pen's made.

(MARION *starts manically sorting through* PEN'S *pile of belongings behind sofa.*)

BOB   Leave it Marion. Everything's fine.

(*Front doorbell rings.*)

MARION   There they are.

BOB   Right. Here we go then. Marion! Come on.

(MARION *and* BOB *exit.*)

PETULA   (*off*) Aaaaaaaaaah! Unbelievable.

MARION   (*off*) Ooooooh. Lovely.

BOB   (*off*) Dougie! Petula!

DOUGIE   (*off*) Look at you, you old bastard!

MARION   (*off*) Go through shall we? Lovely. Lovely.
          Lovely.

          (BOB *and* MARION *enter with* DOUGIE *and* PETULA
          *carrying suitcases and bags. Both expensively
          but tastelessly dressed.* PETULA *wears a strange
          purple coat with matching hat.*)

DOUGIE   Take a look at this! What an apartment mate.

PETULA   Give me a big wet sloppy kiss Bob, you old stick
          in the mud.

          (PETULA *kisses* BOB. MARION *giggles nervously.*)

DOUGIE   Hey! You still do the giggle! Saucy little Marion
          with the dirtiest laugh in Stepney.

MARION   Oh don't!

DOUGIE   You don't look a day over twenty one, sweetheart.

MARION   You haven't changed.

DOUGIE   Though it is getting dark. And the eyesight's not
          what it was.

MARION   Cheeky.

PETULA   Give him a kick in the shin, Marion. Usually does
          the trick.

DOUGIE   Come here, Gorgeous!

          (DOUGIE *picks* MARION *up and spins her round.
          She squeals.*)

BOB   I think I can safely say that time has treated us
          all pretty well.

DOUGIE   You used to have a bit more on top mate. Hey
          Petula — Bob's turned into a slaphead!

          (DOUGIE *slaps* BOB *lightly on his bald patch.*)

MARION   Let me take your coat Petula.

DOUGIE   Look at that view! Petula. Petula come and feast
              your eyes on the panorama.

PETULA   I'm a bit funny about heights Marion. Vertigo.
              Never been fourteen floors up before.

MARION   You'll soon get used to it. Lovely. Such an
              unusual shade of purple.

DOUGIE   It's New York!

BOB   No. It's London.

PETULA   You like it? Little holiday gift from Dougie. All
              the rage back in Oz. Came with the matching hat.

MARION   Lovely.

PETULA   Told him not to. But you know Dougie. He's
              always liked to spoil me.

DOUGIE   What's life about if you can't spoil the little lady
              once in a while. No mate. I mean it looks like
              New York. All the lights and everything. That's
              the Nat West Tower isn't it?

MARION   You can see as far as Highgate on one side and
              Crystal Palace on the other. Come on Petula.
              Come and have a look.

PETULA   You'll have to hold my hand. Feel wobbly being
              so high up.

              (MARION *coaxes* PETULA *onto the balcony.*)

DOUGIE   Crystal Palace, eh? The Who. Open air concert.

PETULA   I'm not sure about this. Oh God! We're in the
              middle of the sky. This balcony. It's not going to
              give way? It is solid?

BOB   I don't know Petula. The original fell off last
              week. Put this one up myself. Made of balsa wood.

PETULA	What!
	(PETULA *runs back inside.*)
MARION	Come on Petula. He's trying to be funny.
	(MARION *coaxes* PETULA *back onto the balcony.*)
BOB	I remember that. Boiling hot day. Sat right at the front by the PA. Deaf for two days after.
MARION	Quite a selling point being up here. Flats go for a good price. Because of the view.
PETULA	It'd have to be because of the view, wouldn't it Marion.
MARION	What do you mean?
PETULA	All the broken windows. The litter. On street level there's not much to shout about.
DOUGIE	Glad to say that's something you don't see in Sydney. People have more respect.
BOB	It's not that bad.
DOUGIE	Take that bloke for example.
BOB	What bloke?
DOUGIE	There. With the alsatian. Letting it do its stuff in the middle of the pathway.
BOB	What. The little . . .
MARION	Why don't we all go inside for now.
DOUGIE	Just wouldn't happen in our neighbourhood.
PETULA	Good idea. My head's spinning.
BOB	OI!
MARION	Bob! It's a bit chilly with evenings drawing in.

(MARION, DOUGIE *and* PETULA *come off the
balcony.* BOB *is more interested in the action
below.*)

BOB   YOU — YES YOU!

MARION   Bob!

(BOB *comes in.* PETULA *finds framed photograph
on the sideboard.*)

PETULA   Is this your little girl? Dougie. Come and have a
            look at the cute little bubby.

MARION   Yes. That's Pen-Pen. School photo.

DOUGIE   What a sweetie. Just like her mother.

MARION   Had a brace on her teeth then. That's why she's
            smiling like her lips are stuck together. Didn't
            want anyone to see the ironmongery.

DOUGIE ⎫   So.
MARION ⎬   Well.
PETULA ⎭   Here we are.

BOB   Right then. How's about a drink?

DOUGIE   Good idea.

MARION   Bob.

BOB   What. Oh Right. Just waiting for. Sorry. Where is
            she?

MARION   Petula. Why don't I show you where you and
            Dougie will be sleeping. Its Pen-Pen's room so
            please excuse the posters. I know Motorhead isn't
            to everyone's taste.

PETULA   Just the two bedrooms. How do you cope?

MARION   Suits our purposes.

(PETULA *and* MARION *exit with bags.* DOUGIE *and*
BOB *size each other up for a moment.*)

DOUGIE   Well my old mucker.

BOB   Dougie me old mate.

            (DOUGIE *and* BOB *hug for as long as machismo
            will allow. Separate and do a few boxing
            movements.* DOUGIE *swaggers over to the display
            cabinet. Picks up a trophy.*)

DOUGIE   Quite a collection of pots you've got here. Still
            winning then.

BOB   You know me.

DOUGIE   Why haven't any of them got inscriptions?

BOB   What?

DOUGIE   What did you do — buy them yourself?

BOB   What. No. No. Ha! Marion. Polishes a lot. Wiped
            them off. You're looking fit Dougie.

            (BOB *steers* DOUGIE *away from the display
            cabinet.*)

DOUGIE   I like to take care of myself. Do a lot of skiing
            these days. Do you ski?

BOB   Ski.

DOUGIE   There are some A-One slopes in Australia. Snobs
            of course like to make out the real McCoy's
            Europe but I'm telling you. You can't beat a
            weekend up in the Snowy mountains. We've got
            it all right on our doorstep.

BOB   Oh we do. I mean we have. Not so much now.
            But. Oh yes. You should see Marion doing
            slalom.

DOUGIE   Where do you go?

BOB   Switzerland. Usually. Yes. Switzerland.

DOUGIE   Gstaad? Lausanne?

BOB   No. The Alps.

DOUGIE   Right you are. The old one-two, eh? Up George's
              gym of a Saturday.

              (DOUGIE *lands a punch in* BOB's *stomach.* BOB
              doubles up and coughs.)

DOUGIE   Alright mate? Not exactly the old washboard
              stomach is it? I'm lucky. Eat what I like. Never
              gain an ounce.

BOB   Bully for you.

DOUGIE   How's work?

BOB   Fine Dougie. Fine. New Governor now. Plenty of
              overtime. We specialise in the classic cars. Get
              some real beauties. Austin Sevens. Standard
              eights. The odd Roller. They don't make them
              like that any more. Engines that sing. Engines
              that sing to you.

DOUGIE   No. Funny. Thought you'd be running the whole
              show by now.

BOB   That's not for me Dougie. I'm a mechanic. Hands
              on man. I belong under a bonnet.

DOUGIE   Glad I don't have to do the grafting any more, I
              can tell you. You've been working at that place
              what, twenty-odd years?

BOB   Twenty six in January.

DOUGIE   Twenty six years. And what have you got to show
              for it, eh?

BOB   We don't go short.

DOUGIE   Don't go short. Listen mate. The birds in the
              trees don't go short. They eat their worms. Sit in
              their nests. But where's the Ferrari? The house by
              the sea? The holidays?

BOB   Don't think your average bluetit lusts after a Ferrari, Dougie.

DOUGIE   What I'm saying, mate. And I don't want you to get me wrong. Is . . . you've got to push yourself ahead, take what you deserve. I have. Twenty six years of sweated labour and you're living in a two bed flat in a tower block. Old banger you got cheap from the workshop — am I right?

BOB   Well. Yes. But Dougie I . . .

DOUGIE   Couldn't even afford to let your Marion come over to Oz when her dear old Auntie Ruby died.

BOB   Eh. Eh. Now just a minute . . .

(BOB *leaps to his feet just as* MARION *and* PETULA *enter from the bedroom.* PETULA *places bag of parcels on floor and jumps into* DOUGIE's *lap.*)

PETULA   You can stop talking about us now. The girlies are back! Dougie. We're sleeping on an air mattress.

DOUGIE   Oh yeah. No room at the inn, eh?

MARION   It's very comfortable.

PETULA   Don't get me wrong Marion. I'm sure it'll be fine. Back home Dougie and me sleep on a water bed. Don't we Bubs?

DOUGIE   That we do, Bubs. That we do. You should give one of those a try Bob. Soon put the wick back in your candle. Ooh. What's that?

(DOUGIE *shifts uncomfortably.*)

BOB   There's plenty of wick in my candle thank you very much.

MARION   Here Dougie. Pop this cushion underneath. There's a spring there that can jump up and catch you unawares.

DOUGIE   Bet you have to watch out, eh Bob? If you're
                anything like you used to be in the posterior
                department.

                (DOUGIE *and* PETULA *laugh*.)

MARION   Petula was showing me her clothes. Designer
                labels. They had to take out special insurance.

BOB   Hmph.

                (*A nasty silence*.)

MARION   You alright Bob?

BOB   Fine thank you.

MARION ⎫   Of course we usually . . .
PETULA ⎰   I was going to let . . .

PETULA   Sorry Marion. After you.

MARION   No. No please.

PETULA   I insist. You are the hostess after all.

BOB   What the hell has happened to Pen-Pen.

MARION   How was the flight?

DOUGIE   Hell. Sixteen hours of hell. I can't go that long
                without a jog, eh Bob?

BOB   Yeah. Of course.

DOUGIE   Stuck in your seat for the best part of a day.

PETULA   We stopped off in Dubai for refuelling.

MARION   Dubai. How exotic. Was it interesting?

PETULA   Not really. Only saw the terminal. Though I did
                get searched.

MARION   Searched?

PETULA   Oh yes. By this big butch women with a moustache and a machine gun slung over her shoulder. Why I don't know. Hardly look terrorist material do I?

MARION   No. Of course not.

PETULA   I mean. Think about it. You name me one criminally minded person who owns a Chanel handbag.

BOB   Imelda Marcos.

(*Silence.*)

MARION   Did they show a film? They do don't they. Show films. On aeroplanes.

PETULA   They do. Yes. But to be honest I didn't pay too much attention. Fill you up with so much free booze. Ended up having a bit of a knees up with this steward from Cirencester. Lovely boy. Used to be a dancer. Must have drunk a bottle of champagne.

MARION   Champagne.

PETULA   Oh yes. On the house. In first. Only in first of course.

BOB   You flew from Australia first class.

DOUGIE   I should say so. Can't have my little lady mixing with the hoipoloi.

BOB   Pity you didn't get any duty-frees.

DOUGIE   What, mate?

BOB   Could have picked up a couple of bottles from the airport. Then we wouldn't be sitting here thirsty.

MARION   Bob!

DOUGIE   Took it for granted you'd have some in. With us being the guests and that.

(*Enter* PEN *with shopping trolley*.)

BOB   Where the bloody hell have you been!

(BOB *dives into the shopping trolley and pulls out two cans of lager. Gives one to* DOUGIE.)

PEN   Nowhere.

MARION   Use glasses Bob. Dougie. A glass.

BOB   I'll give you nowhere. I'll give you . . .

MARION   Stop it Bob.

PETULA   You must be Penelope.

PEN   Pen-Pen. What have I done now?

PETULA   I'm Petula and this is my Dougie.

DOUGIE   Woah Bob. Look like you need that drink.

PETULA   We all go back a long way.

DOUGIE   Taking to the neck oil in your old age.

PEN   So I've heard.

MARION   Did you get the gin Pen-Pen?

DOUGIE   Hello kiddo. Marion. She's the spitting image of you.

PEN   They didn't have any.

BOB   Pen-Pen. Say hello properly.

PEN   Hello properly.

BOB   For God's sake! Excuse our daughter. No manners.

PEN   What is your prob . . .

MARION   Pen-Pen. The gin.

PEN   They were robbed last night. Obviously didn't
         like tequila. Whoever did it. That's all they had
         left.

         (PEN *pulls bottle of tequila from shopping
         trolley.*)

PETULA   Tequila! Ariba! Riba! Riba!

MARION   Lord. Is there anything to mix it with?

PEN   Lemonade.

PETULA   Hey-hey! Don't you remember? Saturday nights
         at the Kipper Klub. That juke box with all the
         glittery records. Slammers! Tequila slammers!
         It's party time!

BOB   The Kipper Klub! I'm with you. You used to put
         that record on again and again. What was it now.

         (BOB *sings the chorus to 'Those Were the Days'
         — The Seekers.*)

BOB   Dada da da dada da da da. . .

MARION   That's right.

         (BOB, MARION, PETULA *and* DOUGIE *all sing.*)

PEN   Oh my God.

PETULA   Come on. Let's set these slammers up, eh?

MARION   Haven't got any lime. But there's lemon. Glasses
         in the cabinet. Bob.

         (*Exit* MARION. BOB *takes four sherry glasses from
         the cabinet.*)

DOUGIE   DON'T FORGET THE SALT, MARION!

PEN   So. Have you ever seen a shark?

PETULA   What?

PEN   Australia. Full of them isn't it?

DOUGIE   The Kipper Klub, Bob. What a joint. Had those
           fish in cases on the walls. Stuffed and varnished.

PETULA   Manly. Our nearest beach. Sit having a sunbake
           and within an hour you'll see the little beggars
           basking about a kilometre out. Never been close.
           Wouldn't be here to tell the tale.

BOB   And the barmaids. Pfff. Weren't hired for their
           brains that's for sure.

DOUGIE   Maybe we shouldn't go into that in front of the
           ladies.

PETULA   Don't mind me. I know what you boys were like.
           In the days when you had hair.

DOUGIE   Hey. Hey. Hey. Don't lump us both in the same
           basket. Bob's the baldy. Here. You had the hots
           for Melissa!

BOB   That's right. Melissa Nobbs. With the forty four
           inch . . .

DOUGIE   You tried your luck didn't you. She poured the
           beerslops over your head and you had to take her
           boyfriend on at closing. Great big bruiser he was.

BOB   Malcolm Prentice. Brains in his biceps.

DOUGIE   Nothing could touch us then, eh? Predatory we
           were. On the hunt.

PEN   So you've never been in the sea and had a shark
           come near you.

PETULA   Oh no. I tend to stick to the pool. Personally.

           (MARION *enters carrying tray with lemon slices
           and salt.*)

DOUGIE   Wey-hey — Here we go!

MARION	Now I think we should be sensible about this.
PETULA	Stuff sensible. We're the four stooges.
BOB	I would like to propose a toast.

(BOB *pours tequila into glasses and stands ready to toast.*)

PEN	You've got a pool. A swimming pool.
DOUGIE	Too right. Fifty by forty, elongated kidney shape. Two boards. Wave simulator. And the latest water filtration system. You could do with a pool, mate. Tone up those muscles.
MARION	Bob. These are sherry glasses.
BOB	To Petula and Dougie, who have travelled halfway around the world to be with us . . .
DOUGIE	Get the snaps out, Bubs. Show the kid the pool.

(PETULA *passes envelope of photographs to* PEN.)

BOB	A lot of water has passed under the bridge. We're all a lot older than we were. But time is a great . . .
MARION	Oh for God's sake Bob, my hand's going to drop off. Come on everyone. Dig in.

(MARION *puts salt on the back of her hand. All follow apart from* BOB *who is miffed.*)

MARION	There's a Tango for you Pen-Pen.
PEN	I'm not thirsty.
MARION	To be sociable. To old friends and old times!
PETULA }	Old friends. Old times.
DOUGIE }	Old friends. Old times.
BOB	Oh. Cheers.

(*All lick salt and drink. A beat. A gasp as the long forgotten sting hits home. All grab for lemon slices.*)

BOB   I'd forgotten how disgusting tequila is.

DOUGIE   Hits home though. Few more of these and you'll be able to cut your leg off without flinching.

MARION   I need a beer after that. Petula?

(MARION *hands* PETULA *a beer and a glass.*)

PETULA   Good idea Marion.

MARION   Stick some of these in the fridge. Pizzery nibbly whatnots should be ready.

(MARION *picks up beers.* BOB *takes two off her.* MARION *exits.*)

PETULA   Enjoying those Pen-Pen?

PEN   This is your house? You really live here?

BOB   Let's have a look.

(PEN *hands* BOB *some photographs.*)

DOUGIE   Like what you see?

PEN   Amazing. Right on the edge of a forest.

PETULA   Get a lot of lizards. Have to check your shoes in the morning or you end up with something slimy between your toes.

DOUGIE   Not bad, eh Bob?

BOB   Bit flash for me Dougie. Don't think I'd paint the front of my house pink.

DOUGIE   Couldn't really could you. They don't make ladders high enough.

PEN   You eat all your meals outside?

PETULA   Sure. When it's hot.

BOB   We can do that here. On the balcony.

PEN   No we can't. You'd end up with carbon monoxide
           poisoning.

DOUGIE   I tell you Pen-Pen. If you like open spaces.
           Wildlife. Australia's the place for you. All kinds
           of snake. Birds. Frogs that grow the size of cats.
           Possums. You name it we've got it. All unspoilt,
           too.

BOB   We do have wildlife of our own you know.

           (BOB *refills glasses with tequila.*)

DOUGIE   Oh yeah.

BOB   Yeah.

DOUGIE   Like what.

BOB   Dogs. You look over the balcony. Any day of the
           week and you can see every conceivable breed of
           dog.

DOUGIE   Not exactly the Garden of Eden is it, mate.

           (MARION *enters with tray on which are plates of
           pizza, cheese straws, sausage rolls, etc.*)

MARION   Its not much. But at least it'll soak up the
           alcohol. Pen-Pen. Hand the plates round.

PETULA   Lovely Marion. I'm a bit peckish.

           (PEN *hands plates round.*)

DOUGIE   Time for another shot girls.

MARION   I don't know Dougie. Feel like I've just drunk
           Domestos.

           (DOUGIE *hands shots round.*)

DOUGIE   This one'll taste better.

              (*All put salt on the back of their hands and lick.*)

PETULA   Prost!
DOUGIE   }   Prost!
BOB   Prost!
MARION   Prost!

DOUGIE   Here, Bubs. Aunty Ruby. Get the . . . Yes?

PETULA   Oh right.

              (PETULA *delves into her bag.*)

MARION   What about Aunty Ruby? Come on Bob. More
              pizza. Hardly anything on your plate.

DOUGIE   Working on the spare tyre, aren't you mate.
              Found it Bubs?

              (PETULA *sits next to* MARION *holding something
              wrapped up in tissue paper.* BOB *opens another
              can of lager.*)

PETULA   Now. Marion. Just before your Aunty Ruby passed
              away. We paid a visit. Went to see her in the
              hospice.

MARION   Aunty Ruby.

PETULA   Very frail of course. And drugged up to the
              eyeballs. But she said how much she missed you.
              That she thought of you all the time. That she
              would have liked to say goodbye.

MARION   Wanted to be there. It was the money.

DOUGIE   We know love. We know.

PETULA   But she . . . well. She said she wanted you to
              have this.

              (PETULA *passes the package to* MARION.)

MARION   Always used to eat pie and mash on a Saturday.
                After shopping. She'd have eels. Suck them
                through the hole in her teeth. She lost all the
                front ones during the war. Slipped on some moss
                and fell on her face running into the Anderson's
                shelter. And in the market she'd buy me a
                Halfpenny'th of lemon sherbets. Made them last
                all week. Always kind to me. Wiped my tears
                away when Mum died. Took me in. Didn't have to.

BOB   Open it up Marion.

                (MARION *takes off tissue wrapping. Holding back
                tears.*)

MARION   And then she went. To Australia.

BOB   What is it?

MARION   It's. It's a . . . it's a stamp collection.

BOB   A what?

                (DOUGIE *bounds over to* MARION *and puts his arm
                around her.* BOB *takes the stamp collection and
                looks at it.*)

DOUGIE   Hey. Hey. Hey. No tears Marion. Where's the
                party girl gone, eh?

BOB   Ancient collection this. Squiggly writing at the
                front. Old fashioned pen.

MARION   Its the tequila. I'll be alright in a minute.

PETULA   Now Dougie and me don't know anything about
                stamps. But there's some really old ones in there.
                Goes way back. Could be worth a few bob.

MARION   We'd never sell it.

DOUGIE   Hang on a minute.

                (DOUGIE *lifts the hair behind* MARION'S *ear.*)

DOUGIE	Your ears still go pink! Hey Petula. Her ears still go pink. One drink and she turns into Dumbo.
MARION	Oh Dougie. I'd forgotten about that.
DOUGIE	That's more like it. The Marion I remember was a happy young girl up for anything. Where's she gone, eh?
BOB	We'll get it valued.

(BOB *puts stamp collection on table.* PEN *looks at it.*)

| MARION | She's still here Dougie. We're not selling it Bob. |

(DOUGIE *refills glasses.*)

| PETULA | Time for the rest of the pressies! Give these Poms a bit of a lift, eh Doug? |

(DOUGIE *hands glasses around. All salt hands as before.* PETULA *hands out presents.*)

PETULA	Bob. That's for you. No. Don't feel it. You'll spoil the surprise. Marion. And of course Pen-Pen.
DOUGIE	Bottoms up and down the hatch!
BOB ⎫ MARION ⎬ PETULA ⎭	Down the hatch! Down the hatch! Down the hatch!

(*All grab lemon slices.* BOB *belches loudly.*)

BOB	Pardon me.
PETULA	Come on then. What are we waiting for?
MARION	Open mine first shall I? Really didn't expect presents Petula. Just lovely to see you both.

(MARION *opens her present. A large lurid orange koala print piece of material.*)

| MARION | Oh. Oh its lovely. Lovely. Isn't it lovely Bob? |

BOB   Lovely.

MARION   Orange. Lovely. Funnily enough we don't have
            much in orange. Koala bears too. Lovely. Always
            in need of a tablecloth.

PETULA   Oh Marion. It isn't a tablecloth. Its a sarong.
            Vital part of any Australian wardrobe.

MARION   A sarong?

PETULA   Stand up. I'll show you how to put it on. Quite a
            knack to it.

MARION   You wear it. This. I mean . . . lovely.

            (MARION *stands and* PETULA *ties sarong over*
            MARION'S *dress*.)

DOUGIE   What are you waiting for Pen-Pen. Open yours
            up. Got a hunch you're going to like it.

BOB   I think another would go down nicely. What do
            you say Dougie?

DOUGIE   Drink you under the table any day of the week.

BOB   No competition mate. Marion?

MARION   I think Petula and I will pass on this one Bob.

PETULA   Speak for yourself. Set me one up sweetheart.

            (BOB *refills glasses*.)

MARION   Well. What do you think?

PETULA   Give the boys a twirl Marion.

            (BOB *hands shots to* PETULA *and* DOUGIE.)

DOUGIE   What a knockout, eh Bob?

BOB   Cheers!

PETULA }   Cheers.
DOUGIE }   Cheers.

MARION   Bob?

BOB   Very. Very colourful love.

PEN   This is unbelievable. Incredible.

BOB   That hit the spot alright.

PEN   Wow.

DOUGIE   Did it? Can't even feel it, mate.

MARION   What have you got Pen-Pen?

PEN   A CD Walkman. A really good CD Walkman.
            With an LCD display and a case and . . . wow.

BOB   A what?

MARION   Oh Petula. Dougie. Pen-Pen really can't accept that!

PEN   Yes I can.

MARION   It's far too expensive.

DOUGIE   I pick them up cost price from a contact in the
            Far East. You like it kiddo?

PEN   I've never had anything like this before.
            Brilliant. Thanks.

BOB   CD's cost an arm and a leg.

DOUGIE   Don't be a misery Bob. We'll pick up a few CD's
            for the kid when we go into town tomorrow.

PETULA   Yeah. What music you into Pen-Pen. How's about
            Take That? They look a lovely bunch of fellas.
            Seen the photos. Or . . . who is it? Dougie . . . oh
            . . . graffiti everywhere. In the lift. The hallway.
            Figure they must be pretty big. In our day it was
            the Stones. But . . . er . . . no . . . what is it?
            BNP! That's it — BNP! Forever! You into the
            BNP?

PEN	No I'm not.
PETULA	Not your sort of sound, eh?
PEN	No. The BNP is a fascist political party.
PETULA	Strewth. Things have changed around here. Seems a pretty glum place to be growing up in.
BOB	I'll buy my daughter CD's thank you.
PEN	It is.
DOUGIE	Enjoy it sweetie. Your Dad's always been a bit of a grouch.
BOB	I have not.
DOUGIE MARION } PETULA	You have. You have. You have.
MARION	Outvoted Bob.
PETULA	Oh come on Bobby. Don't go sulky. Still ticklish are we? Um?
	(PETULA *tickles* BOB.)
BOB	Stop it. Get off!
PETULA	Only if you open up your pressie. Come on.
BOB	Alright. Alright.
	(BOB *takes off one layer of wrapping to find another. He tries to rip through the whole package.*)
PETULA	No you don't Bob. One layer at a time. Took ages to do up. Maybe it'll be the next one.
	(BOB *takes off another layer.*)
DOUGIE	Got to keep on trying. You don't get something for nothing in this life.

MARION	What have you got Bob?
BOB	About eight sheets of paper.
PETULA	Nearly there.

(BOB *takes off another layer to reveal nothing.*)

PETULA	Ah. Shame.
BOB	Very funny.
DOUGIE	See. You are a grouch.
BOB	I am not a grouch.

(BOB *gets to his present. A boomerang. He stares at it.*)

BOB	A boomerang.
DOUGIE	Not just any old boomerang. That boomerang comes from the Aboriginal reservation just outside Wagga Wagga. The genuine article.
MARION	It's beautiful. Look at those carvings. Isn't it lovely Bob?
PETULA	Why don't you give it a go?
BOB	What?
DOUGIE	Yeah mate. Come on. Out here. You've got the air space.
PETULA	Here we go!

(DOUGIE *and* BOB *go unsteadily onto the balcony.*)

MARION	Bob. Be careful.
BOB	What I want to know. Right. And I want your assurance on this. Is. Will it come back?
DOUGIE	Sure it will. No doubt about it.

BOB	Hundred per cent. Hundred per cent sure.
DOUGIE	As eggs are eggs, mate.
BOB	Ok.
MARION	Bob.
BOB	You do it.
DOUGIE	Me?
BOB	You do it. Then I'll have a go.
MARION	It's deceptive. The other block's a lot closer than you think.
PETULA	Come on Dougie baby. Show us how it's done.
MARION	Could always go down to the communal gardens.
DOUGIE	Ok. Hand it over. Now. It's all down to the throwing motion see. Got to get the lift underneath so it goes in a nice gentle arc. Like this.
BOB	Right.
DOUGIE	Ready. And a one. And a two and a three!
	(DOUGIE *throws boomerang. All follow its course.*)
PETULA	Look. Look, it's turning back. It's . . .
MARION	Mind the balcony doors.
	(DOUGIE *catches the returning boomerang. All clap.*)
PEN	Cool.
PETULA	Well done Bubs.
BOB	Very impressive.
MARION	Yes. Seen it now. Lovely. Come inside shall we?

DOUGIE   Bob's got to have a go. Unless you'd rather leave
                it to the expert, eh?

BOB   Give it here.

DOUGIE   Remember. Catch the lift. Use the curve.

BOB   One . . .

PETULA   There's an old saying.

PEN ⎫   Two . . .
MARION ⎬   Two . . .
DOUGIE ⎭   Two . . .

PETULA   A boomerang only comes back if it wants to come
                back.

BOB ⎫   Three!
PEN ⎪   Three.
MARION ⎬   Three.
DOUGIE ⎭   Three.

                (BOB *throws the boomerang.*)

PETULA   If the spirit is with you.

                (*Sound of breaking glass.*)

MARION   Oh my God!

PETULA   Oh dear. Obviously lacking in the spirit
                department.

BOB   Soon make up for that.

                (BOB *storms inside and pours himself glass of
                tequila. Lights cigarette.*)

MARION   Inside. Everyone. Right now. Before someone
                sees us.

BOB   Its alright. That flat's empty.

PEN   You ought to report it.

MARION   Bloody silly thing to do. You could have hurt someone.

DOUGIE   Tough luck Bob. You've lost your boomerang.

MARION   You've had more than enough.

            (BOB *downs his tequila and refills all the glasses.*)

BOB   Gust of wind. Blew it off course.

PEN   You ought to tell the council. Or the police'll get someone else for it.

BOB   Whose side are you on?

PEN   Just don't think its right.

BOB   Pay your way and you can tell me what's right and wrong.

PEN   I'm entitled to an opinion.

BOB   Only if it's the right one.

PEN   Don't shout at me because you're angry with him.

MARION   Stop it, the pair of you. Pen-Pen. Make yourself useful. Take the plates out.

BOB   And beer. Bring some more beer while you're at it.

PEN   What did your last servant die of?

            (*Exit* PEN *with plates on tray.*)

PETULA   Still work at that pub, Marion?

MARION   The odd shift. Only its not a pub now. Its a Tex Mex entertainment complex. I have to wear a sombrero and set up the bucking bronco but it's basically bar work.

DOUGIE   I'm glad my Petula doesn't go out to work. I like her at home warming my cockles, eh Bubs.

PETULA   Oh Dougie.

MARION   I don't mind Dougie. Gets me out. Can feel very
           isolated round here. I'd rather do that than sit on
           my bum all day.

PETULA   I don't sit on my bum all day Marion. I do charity
           work.

MARION   Oh yes.

PETULA   At the hospital. In the shop mainly but sometimes
           I pop up to the wards to perk the patients up a
           bit. Learn a lot, too. About ailments. Not much I
           don't know about ingrowing toenails and hernias.

MARION   Bob had a hernia last year. Took him nine
           months to get the operation. That was after being
           turned away four times because there weren't any
           beds.

DOUGIE   Now that just wouldn't happen in Oz. Even under
           the Medicare system. Though we're private now
           of course.

BOB   Of course.

           (PEN *enters with several beers.* BOB *takes one.*)

DOUGIE   Hey Pen-Pen. How's about some sounds eh? Make
           an old man happy. Shake a leg with a geriatric.

           (DOUGIE *grabs* PEN *and dances around her.*)

BOB   Sounds?

PETULA   Ignore him Pen-Pen. Couple of beers inside him
           and he thinks he's Mel Gibson and Fred Astaire
           rolled into one.

DOUGIE   Where's your hi-fi?

           (DOUGIE *spots the stereo/radio and fiddles with
           it.*)

PETULA   Maybe we should go out. Up the boozer. Lets
            have an adventure eh?

BOB   Have another beer.

DOUGIE   There's something wrong with your motor, mate.

PETULA   Here — have you still got Twister? The mat with
            the coloured circles. And you try not to fall over.
            Remember we used to play it in your mum and
            dad's front room.

BOB   What? Pen-Pen, what have you done to the
            stereo?

            (PETULA *pours more tequila into glasses.* MARION
            delves into the bottom of the sideboard.)

MARION   Now unless I'm very much mistaken . . .

PEN   I haven't done anything to the stereo. Haven't
            played it in weeks. Always going on at me
            because it's too loud.

PETULA   Walked in on us didn't they. Thought we were
            having some sort of orgy.

MARION   Here we are. See if it's all . . . yes. Look.

            (MARION *opens Twister box and takes out mat.*)

DOUGIE   It's an old machine. They don't last forever.

PETULA   Lay it out, Marion. Come on.

PEN   Yeah. Exactly. Tell him.

BOB   It's two years old. You've been overplaying.

PETULA   I think we are all in desperate need of another
            shot!

            (PETULA *hands around shots.*)

PEN   It's crap anyway. Sounds like the music's coming
            out of a dustbin. All echoey and tinny.

BOB   Turning into a stereo snob are we? Since we've
               moved into the CD Walkman bracket. Spoiled
               brat.

PEN   Bloody hell.

DOUGIE   Planned obsolescence, that's what it is.

BOB   What did you say?

DOUGIE   Made to pack up after a while. So you buy
               another one. Have you got a screwdriver mate?

               (BOB *looks in drawer for screwdriver.*)

PETULA   Ariba!

DOUGIE ⎫   Ariba!
MARION ⎭   Ariba! — Bob.

BOB   What? Oh Ariba, yeah. Here.

               (BOB *hands* DOUGIE *screwdriver.* PETULA *chases
               her tequila with beer. She spills some.*)

PETULA   Butterfingers. Sorry about the carpet, Marion. I
               dribbled.

MARION   It's alright. I bought it beer-coloured. Bob
               dribbles too.

               (MARION *and* PETULA *giggle.*)

PEN   What's so funny about that?

MARION   Let your hair down Pen-Pen. Have another
               Tango.

PEN   You're drunk.

MARION   Merry is the polite term.

DOUGIE   Come on then boys and girls. What do we do for
               fun around here?

BOB	I don't know.
DOUGIE	What do you usually do?
PETULA	Let's play Twister!
MARION	Maybe later. My co-ordination's up the spout.
BOB	Get a take-away once in a while. A video.
PETULA	Don't you have parties? Me and Dougie have loads of parties. Barbies at the weekend. By the pool.
MARION	Bob doesn't like parties.
BOB	We never get invited to any.
DOUGIE	Mr Popularity, eh?
BOB	I mean there's no one round here to have parties with. Most of the old crowd have moved out to Essex.
PETULA	What about the neighbours?
MARION	What about the neighbours.
PETULA	Surely you meet up for a gossip. Chew the fat.
MARION	Don't know the neighbours. Never seen them really. Bob shouts obscenities at them from the balcony every now and again but that's about it.
PETULA	But that's awful. Don't you think that's awful Dougie?
DOUGIE	Typical Brit behaviour. Xenophobia.
BOB	What.
DOUGIE	Uptight. Held in. Shut off.
BOB	Listen. If someone made the effort we'd meet them halfway. Isn't that right Marion?
MARION	Yes. That's right Bob.

PETULA   Well. Well. That is it then! That's it!

MARION   What? What's what?

BOB   People round here keep themselves to themselves.
           It's safer that way.

PETULA   Excuses. It's all excuses. No! Bobby. Marion. I'm
           going to do you a favour. I'm going next door.
           Right now. I'm going next door and I'm going to
           ask your neighbours in for a nice sociable
           friendly drink.

BOB   You're what?

MARION   But . . . but we don't know who they are. Could
           be anyone.

PETULA   You said it. Someone made the effort . . .

MARION   Complete strangers.

PETULA   You'd meet them halfway. Well. I'm making the
           effort for you. You can make friends. Become
           acquainted.

DOUGIE   Good on you, Bubs. Bring 'em in! Bring 'em all in!

PETULA   Bobby. Marion. You are going to thank me for this.

           (*Exit* PETULA.)

BOB   Not really going to do it, is she?

DOUGIE   'Course she is mate.

BOB   Bloody hell.

MARION   I hope there aren't too many of them. Hardly any
           food left. Suppose it's a great big family.
           Children. Grandparents.

DOUGIE   Then you explain. Spur of the moment thing you
           say. With any luck they'll bring their own
           provisions. Back home we always make sure

we've got a six-pack and few steaks in the
freezer. Just in case we get asked to a barbie.

BOB   Well let's hope they do. Bring their own
             provisions. We can't feed the five thousand.

MARION   Quite exciting really isn't it?

DOUGIE   You see Bob. Marion's got the right idea. Open
             your mind. Open your heart. Open your house.
             We're all just one big brotherhood of human
             beings!

             (PETULA *enters, swaying slightly.*)

PETULA   Bob. Marion. Pen-Pen. I would like you to meet
             your neighbour. Trevor!

             (PETULA *stands back.* TREVOR *enters. An
             immensely threatening figure. Hollow-eyed and
             dangerous looking.* BOB *springs to his feet and
             moves instinctively towards* MARION *and* PEN. *A
             stunned silence.*)

PEN   You know that pop group you were talking about?
             He sings backing vocals.

             (BOB *approaches* TREVOR.)

BOB   Trevor. Er. Trevor. My name's Bob.

TREVOR   Bob. B.O.B. Bob. Rhymes with knob.

BOB   Oh. Yes. Er. Yes. Ha! So it does. Well if it helps
             to . . . an aide memoire, so to speak. Then
             terrific. Um. How about a beer?

TREVOR   Tequila.

BOB   Tequila? Yes. A tequila. Get into the party spirit,
             eh. By all means.

             (BOB *pours an inch of tequila into tumbler.*)

TREVOR   More.

BOB   More. Yes. Yes. Of course. Big lad like you.
           Hollow legs no doubt.

           (BOB *pours more into tumbler.* TREVOR *motions
           for more until tumbler is full and bottle drained.*
           BOB *picks up can of lager.*)

BOB   There you go. Have a chaser. Terrific. I was
           going to say if . . . I mean. Terrific really. But
           . . . er . . . Dougie and Petula here. Well . . . you
           know. . . They're from Australia . . . different
           world. Spur of the moment thing. But . . . well . . .
           if you're in the middle of, I don't know . . .
           dinner . . . favourite programme . . . Ha! Basket
           weaving — who knows. Then please feel free . . .
           please . . . no obligation. Welcome of course.
           Terrific! But do feel free at any time . . . to go.

           (TREVOR *drains his glass and twitches violently,
           causing* BOB *to jump back.*)

BOB   Ha!

           (TREVOR *takes a slow methodical walk around the
           room seemingly sizing everything up.*)

MARION   I . . . I suppose your flat is more or less identical
           Trevor. All the same in this block.

TREVOR   No. This is nice. Very nice. Like a home.

MARION   Oh. Thank you. Thank you.

DOUGIE   On your own next door, mate?

TREVOR   Mostly.

BOB   Mostly?

TREVOR   Apart from Wednesdays. Wednesdays my social
           worker comes round.

MARION   Oh yes.

TREVOR	Checks me out. Makes sure I'm stable. That I've been taking it.
BOB	Taking what?
TREVOR	My medication.

(BOB *and* MARION *exchange glances.*)

PETULA	But you've got a little doggy haven't you. That must be company.
TREVOR	Yeah.
PETULA	Came up and licked my hand. Lovely little thing.
TREVOR	Some people though. Some people don't like dogs. Call you names.
DOUGIE	They call you names for having a dog?
TREVOR	Yeah.
PETULA	Like what?
TREVOR	Beanpole.

(BOB *squirms.*)

MARION	Trevor. Have a cheese straw. Look like you could do with feeding up. Petula — more beer. Dougie. You need a refill.

(MARION *replenishes everyone's drink while making desperate 'get rid of him' gestures to* BOB.)

TREVOR	Alright?
PEN	Alright.
BOB	You two know each other?
TREVOR	Fat Philip. Closed the snooker club. All boarded up. He's gone.
PEN	I know. Everyone goes. Eventually.

BOB   What's going on?

PETULA   Pen-Pen you're a dark horse. Do I sense a
               romance in the air?

MARION   Shut up Petula. You're drunk.

PETULA   What.

DOUGIE   Steady on Marion.

               (TREVOR *moves to display cabinet. Eyes the cups.*)

TREVOR   Tarnished. Should polish them up. All yellow.

               (BOB *dives in.*)

BOB   They're plate. All of them. Worthless. Junk.
               Throwing them away.

               (TREVOR *ambles over to* PEN'S *CD player.*)

TREVOR   Tasty. Very tasty. Digital display. Hundred and
               fifty quid at least.

DOUGIE   Know anything about stamps, mate?

MARION   Dougie!

BOB   For God's sake.

DOUGIE   Only we brought this collection over for Marion
               here and none of us have got a clue.

               (TREVOR *walks over to table. Sits and looks
               through the collection.*)

PETULA   Hobby of yours Trevor?

TREVOR   No.

BOB   Oh. Well in that case I don't think . . .

               (BOB *tries to take collection from* TREVOR — *he
               hangs on to it.*)

TREVOR	But I've read a lot of books. About stamps. The library was full of them. Inside.
MARION	Inside! Bob.
TREVOR	Penny Blue.
DOUGIE	What mate?
TREVOR	You've got a Penny Blue. Dead rare.
BOB	Penny Blue. What — like a Penny Black?
TREVOR	Same time. Yeah. The blues were two pence stamps. 1884. Post just starting. Men in top hats. Coach and four. Penny Blue. Sweet.
BOB	Is it worth anything?
TREVOR	Oh yeah.
BOB	Well. How much. How much is it worth?
TREVOR	Depends.
BOB	On what?
TREVOR	Who you go to. Its unused. Good condition.
BOB	Roughly. Give us a rough guess.
TREVOR	About five grand.
MARION	Five thousand pounds! Bob. Bob.

(BOB *picks up the stamp collection and puts it on top of the display cabinet.*)

MARION	Ah. I think we could do with some more beer. Oh yes. Bob love. Bob could you . . .
BOB	What?
MARION	Come and help me with the . . . with the . . .
BOB	What?

MARION   The . . . er . . . needs a . . . on the . . .

BOB   Eh?

MARION   Just come with me will you.

            (MARION *pulls* BOB *who is reluctant to leave the
            stamp collection. They exit.*)

DOUGIE   So. Trevor. What's your line?

TREVOR   Demolition.

DOUGIE   Oh right. Labouring.

TREVOR   Explosives.

PETULA   My goodness. Get much call for that in these
            parts?

TREVOR   Used to. Don't blow things up so much now. Just
            let them stand there until they fall to pieces.
            Cheaper that way. Haven't had a job for two
            years.

            (*Sound of plate breaking and muffled shouting in
            the kitchen.*)

            Round here they take things apart bit by bit. High
            density building. Sixties. Built everything on top
            of each other. No space for big bangs. So they're
            taking it down brick by brick. Like legoland.
            Legoland in reverse.

            (MARION *and* BOB *enter flustered.* BOB *checks
            position of stamp collection.*)

PEN   Trevor blows things up for a living.

MARION   Oh. Lovely.

PETULA   We were saying Trevor. People around here are
            so unfriendly these days. Now once upon a time
            folk left their doors open. All and sundry
            wandering in and out. Don't understand what
            everyone's so afraid of.

TREVOR   Murder I s'pose.

BOB   Right. Right. Right. Trevor. Young lad about
           town. Probably got something lined up. Friday
           night and all that. Out with your mates. Pull the
           birds. We know what it's like don't we Dougie.

DOUGIE   That we do Bob. That we do.

TREVOR   No.

BOB   Don't want to cramp your style.

TREVOR   I'm fine here.

BOB   Cooped up with a bunch of oldies.

TREVOR   You trying to get rid of me?

BOB ⎫   Oh no. No. No. Its just we . . . oh no.
MARION ⎭   No of course not. No of course we don't.

MARION   Bob.

BOB   We're going out.

DOUGIE   We are?

PETULA   Yippee!

BOB   Yes. The pub. Fancy a drink, eh Petula?

PETULA   Mine's a large one.

BOB   Terrific.

PETULA   With a cherry on top and a packet of porkie
           scratchings.

BOB   Marion. Coats please.

           (MARION *exits.* BOB *expects* TREVOR *to move. He
           doesn't.*)

BOB   Soon. Going I mean. Sooner rather than later.
           Yes. Maybe now actually. Yes. Dougie. Like we
           arranged.

DOUGIE   I don't know what you're talking about mate.

TREVOR   I'll come with you.

           (MARION *returns with coats.*)

BOB   What?

DOUGIE   You can count me out.

TREVOR   Need some cigarettes.

           (BOB *helps* PETULA *put her coat on.*)

PETULA   Bobby sweetheart. I can see two of you. Two Bobs
           for the price of one.

BOB   Marion. Put your coat on.

MARION   I don't know Bob. That I can be bothered. You go
           ahead.

BOB   Oh. Oh. Right then. Trevor.

           (TREVOR *stands.*)

TREVOR   (*to* MARION) Thanks for the drink.

           (TREVOR *walks over to* BOB. *He twitches again.*)

BOB   Oh my God.

TREVOR   Take care of the Penny Blue. Wouldn't want to
           get it nicked. Cheers.

           (*Exit* TREVOR, BOB *and* PETULA.)

MARION   Trevor is not the sort of person you want to invite
           into your home Dougie.

DOUGIE   Oh come on Marion.

MARION   Only hope they'll be alright.

DOUGIE   'Course they will. Bob can take care of himself. Hasn't changed, has he? Never was any good at telling porky pies was he?

MARION   I happen to think that's a virtue.

            (BOB *re-appears.*)

BOB   (*whispering*) We'll just pop into the Falstaff. Shake him off in five minutes.

DOUGIE   What have you done with my Petula, mate?

BOB   She's in the lift. Leaning against the button. Keeping the door open.

MARION   With him?

BOB   Five minutes.

            (BOB *exits.*)

PEN   Shall I go with them. In case they fall over.

MARION   You stay here Pen-Pen. No point in everyone going out unnecessarily. If you want to do me a favour you can make Dougie and Petula's bed up.

PEN   Great.

            (PEN *exits.*)

DOUGIE   Might as well have another crack at this.

            (DOUGIE *picks up the stereo/radio and the screwdriver.*)

MARION   You can stop wondering Dougie. Dates are all wrong. She isn't yours.

DOUGIE   Eh. What? No. I didn't think. Listen, Marion that was a long time ago.

MARION   I've seen you looking at her. Doing your sums. No need. Can tell the moment she opens her

mouth. Just like him. From her stubbornness to
the way her toenails curl inward. Two peas in a
pod. Reason they don't get on I suppose. So
forget it Dougie. Madness anyway. Night before
me and Bob got married. You had rust on your
bell-bottoms from shinning up the drainpipe.
Made out it was some sort of mercy mission. Bob
had sent you over to make sure I hadn't passed
out with pre-wedding nerves.

DOUGIE   That's true. He had.

MARION   Shared half a bottle of bacardi and fell onto the
            patchwork guilt. Not exactly moonlight and roses.

DOUGIE   Marion. I've forgotten it.

MARION   Good.

DOUGIE   In just as much detail as you.

MARION   Stop it Dougie. Do you hear me? I don't love you.
            I didn't love you then and I don't love you now.

DOUGIE   Never loved you either.

MARION   Glad to hear it.

DOUGIE   We're square then. We both hate each other.

            (MARION *laughs*.)

DOUGIE   There's that giggle again.

MARION   Here's to you Dougie.

            (MARION *raises her glass*.)

DOUGIE   And to you love. And to you. You're lucky
            Marion.

MARION   Me? Lucky? Don't make me laugh.

DOUGIE   To have Pen-Pen. Notice it as you get older.
            Think it must be comforting to have a kid.
            Something to cheer you up in your dotage.

MARION   You're a long way off that Dougie. Why didn't
            you and Petula . . . if you don't mind my asking.

DOUGIE   Fellopians. Tubes like the barrel of a replica rifle.
            Completely blocked. Anyway. Petula's not keen
            on kids. Get in the way of the good times. Make a
            mess.

MARION   You can't have it all Dougie. You've got the
            dream lifestyle.

DOUGIE   And you've got the kid. Quits.

MARION   Quits.

DOUGIE   Now. If we just plug this baby in. We should be
            ready for . . .

            (DOUGIE *plugs the stereo in. Radio plays 'Come
            Fly With Me' — Frank Sinatra.*)

MARION   You've fixed it. Its working!

DOUGIE   Not only is it working but its ol' Blue Eyes
            himself, Marion sweetheart. May I have the
            honour?

MARION   Oh Dougie.

DOUGIE   Come on.

            (MARION *and* DOUGIE *dance drunkenly around the
            room.* DOUGIE *tries some fancy footwork and both
            he and* MARION *collapse on the sofa. They are
            very close.*)

MARION   Oh Dougie.

            (*Enter* BOB.)

BOB   What the . . .

DOUGIE   Woah! Alright mate.

(DOUGIE *springs to his feet.* MARION *straightens herself up.*)

MARION   Bob. Didn't see you there.

BOB   I gathered that.

DOUGIE   Where's Petula?

BOB   Concerned about your wife are you? Seem to be more interested in mine.

MARION   Bob. Don't get aggressive. We've all had a lot to drink.

BOB   Your wife is lying on the bathroom floor with her feet in the sink demanding that we play Twister. Nipped into the Gents in the pub. Came out and she was singing 'I Will Survive' on the kareoke, smiling and waving at Trevor who now seems to be her best friend in the whole world.

MARION   Best check she's alright.

DOUGIE   She'll be fine.

(MARION *exits.*)

DOUGIE   She saw this video about avoiding varicose veins by sticking your legs in the air. Always does it when she's had a few.

(DOUGIE *makes to go but* BOB *stops him.*)

BOB   Hold your horses Don Giovanni. I want a word with you.

DOUGIE   Come on mate, you're a bit squiffy. Can't it wait 'til morning?

BOB   No. No it bloody can't. One. One. This. This here is my flat. Might not be much. No swimming pool. No lizards in the garden.

DOUGIE   There isn't a garden.

Bob	You're right. There isn't a garden. And there aren't any lizards. But this is my home. And an Englishman's home is his castle.
Dougie	Why don't you sit down before you fall over?
Bob	Two. Two. I resent your wife inviting just anyone in here willy nilly. Opening us up to danger.
Dougie	There's no harm . . .
Bob	And three! You can keep your dirty paws off my Marion!
Dougie	All entirely innocent. Misread the situation mate.
Bob	And four.
Dougie	Four?
Bob	Why do you talk with that bloody phoney Australian accent.
Dougie	What?
Bob	Coming over here with your how's it going mate and your neck oil and all the Crocodile Dundee business. You're more Englisher than I am. You were a phoney when you were younger and you're a phoney now you're older and you get right up my nose. I'll tell you that for nothing.

(Pen *enters.*)

Pen	What's all the shouting about?
Bob	And you can shut up too.
Dougie	Ok. Bob. Ok. Maybe Petula was a bit forward asking the young fella in. But she didn't know what he'd be like.
Bob	No. No she didn't. That's just my point. He was walking around casing the joint! And you Missy. What are you doing hanging around with that

sort of lowlife? That what you get up to is it?
Disappearing for hours on end.

PEN   Seen him that's all. I don't hang around with him.

BOB   Standing on street corners behaving like a tramp.

DOUGIE   Leave the girl alone, Bob.

BOB   Won't pull your finger out. Oh no. Quite content
          to bleed me dry. Well. That's it. Enough. You
          can kiss goodbye to any notion of that bloody day
          trip. That is out. You hear me? Out.

PEN   What? Why? I haven't done anything.

DOUGIE   Thought you were having a go at me, Bob.

BOB   Earn your own money pay for your own day trips!

PEN   You rotten old bastard.

BOB   What? What? Come here and say that.

          (BOB *advances on* PEN.)

DOUGIE   Why don't you dry up! Going off your rocker
          because a stranger's walked onto your patch. No
          sense of adventure. Haven't changed have you.

BOB   What?

DOUGIE   You heard.

BOB   No sense of adventure? I'll give you a sense of
          adventure on the end of your nose in a minute.

          (BOB *rolls up his sleeves.* MARION *enters.*)

BOB   I'll see your neck as long as my arm.

MARION   Petula isn't feeling very well.

DOUGIE   Neither am I. There's a nasty smell in here.

MARION   Pull your sleeves down Bob. Look like you're
          about to do the washing up.

BOB   Spent four hours in the nick out on a limb for
             you. So don't tell me I haven't got a sense of
             adventure.

DOUGIE   Oh here we go. Time to crack open the old
             chestnuts.

MARION   Bob. You promised me.

PEN   What's going on?

BOB   I'll tell you what's going on. Dougie here. Good
             old Dougie, the returning hero, landed your old
             man right in it. Sitting on his backside in an
             aeroplane while I was standing in an identity
             parade.

PEN   What?

DOUGIE   You got off didn't you?

BOB   Safe as houses you said. No chance of getting
             caught. Packing your suitcase while muggins here
             was passing forged postal orders across the
             counter so bad the ink was coming off on my
             fingers.

DOUGIE   If you hadn't blabbed your mouth off in every pub
             this side of the city you wouldn't have had your
             collar felt. All your own stupid fault.

BOB   And you weren't stupid were you. Oh no. You
             knew what you were about. Taking off to
             Australia.

DOUGIE   We'd been planning that for months.

BOB   Upholding a tradition I suppose. Been sending
             our scum over there for centuries.

MARION   Bob!

DOUGIE   You listen to me Bob Butler. Brought all your
            problems on yourself. God knows how Marion
            puts up with your petty little tantrums.

BOB   You leave Marion out of it.

DOUGIE   Completely mismanaged everything you've laid
            your hands on. Never amounted to anything
            because your bloody pig-headedness got in the
            way. You've screwed up mate and you're taking
            it out on the world. Don't be a loser all your life.
            Take a day off.

BOB   I'll give you loser, you . . .

            (BOB *punches* DOUGIE *who lands on Twister mat.*)

MARION   Bob! What have you done! Dougie?

            (MARION *tends to* DOUGIE.)

BOB   (*to* PEN) What are you staring at? Sick of the
            sight of you.

DOUGIE   My nose. I think you've busted my nose.

BOB   (*to* PEN) Why don't you clear off?

PEN   Where to. Haven't even got a room to go to.

            (PETULA *enters.*)

MARION   Shut up! Just shut up! All of you! I've had
            enough.

PETULA   Great. We are playing Twister after all!

            (*Blackout.*)

ACT TWO

The same. The following afternoon.

Slight signs of disturbance. A lamp has been knocked over. A few books pulled out of their place.

DOUGIE *sits in his jacket surrounded by shopping bags. He has a plaster over the bridge of his nose and a black eye.* PETULA *parades up and down wearing a Union Jack apron, carrying a Union Jack umbrella and wearing a Union Jack tea cosy on her head.*

PETULA   (*singing*) 'Rule Britannia. Britannia rules the waves. Britons never never never shall be slaves.'

DOUGIE   Very good sweetheart. Just hope we've got room for it all.

PETULA   I thought the cosy for Val and Alf. The brolly'll be handy for Ross on his fishing trips. And Veronica must, must, *must* have the apron. You know what a sloppy cook she is. Can practically eat your dinner off her scoop neck after she's had a session with the pots and pans.

DOUGIE   Bit much when you can't park your car outside your own flat, eh Petula?

PETULA   He's got a permit. Someone took his space.

DOUGIE   Could murder a cuppa.

PETULA   Best wait for Marion. You know what she's like with her kitchen. Move a pepperpot and she comes out in a nervous rash. Certainly done some walking today. Feet are killing me.

DOUGIE   Can't say my faceache is much improved. Bob can still throw a healthy punch.

PETULA   That's a nasty bruise, Bubs. What on earth did you say to make him do that?

DOUGIE   I told you A few home truths. Let's leave it at
          that. You know what he's like. Short fuse. And
          he'd had a skinful. Far too much singing syrup.

          (DOUGIE *walks out onto the balcony*.)

PETULA   I don't remember much. Bit of a blur. I hope I
          didn't embarrass myself.

          (PETULA *goes through her shopping*.)

DOUGIE   No worries, Bubs. You were fine. These Brits
          don't know how to enjoy themselves. I tell you I
          couldn't live back here. No way. Not for a million
          bucks. Knew it was changing when we left. Never
          thought it'd go so far. Rotten housing. Rotten
          facilities. Docklands on one side. City on the
          other. And this forgotten patch in the middle.
          Madness. Like surrounding a kid with toffees and
          tying him into his pram. If there's got to be poor
          folk they should at least stick them somewhere
          they can't see how green the grass is on the other
          side. Asking for trouble. They should raze the
          place to the ground and start again. Somewhere
          fresh.

PETULA   That little incident outside the theatre. "Petula —
          please inform Dougie that I will pay for my wife
          to see *Les Miserables* thank you very much."
          You'd think you were making some sort of
          proposition.

DOUGIE   His bed, Bubs. He's got to roll around in it.

PETULA   It's the kid I feel sorry for. Growing up around
          here. Bob jumping down her throat every minute.
          If I had a little girl I wouldn't behave like that.

DOUGIE   All very well to talk. Just don't know do we. Who
          needs kids, eh? Couldn't do what we do out by the
          pool with a bunch of sprogs hanging around, eh?

PETULA   Dougie! You know I don't condone that sort of
          behaviour.

DOUGIE   You love it. Especially if you think the
             MacKenzies are watching next door.

             (PETULA *lifts up a very expensive but utterly
             disgusting dress.*)

PETULA   That is your warped fantasy. Not mine. Now. Will
             it do? Sort of regal with a touch of the Caribbean.
             Got to make the effort. It is the Royal
             Shakespeare Company after all.

DOUGIE   Don't know how much more culture I can take.
             Theatre twice in one day. I'll be an intellectual
             before I know it.

PETULA   Dougie.

             (PETULA *sidles up to* DOUGIE *and sits on his lap.*)

DOUGIE   Yeah.

PETULA   You are going to make it up with Bobby aren't you?

DOUGIE   Petula.

PETULA   Couple more hours and we'll be out of here. And . . .

DOUGIE   I don't know why we couldn't have left this
             morning.

PETULA   We can't leave with a bad taste in our mouths.

DOUGIE   Oh I don't know.

PETULA   So silly. You two haven't said a civil word to
             each other all day.

DOUGIE   Hasn't given me a chance. He's not talking to me
             is he?

PETULA   Try. Whatever it is just tell him he's completely
             right and you're completely wrong. If he's
             anything like the Bobby of old he'll fall for it
             hook line and sinker.

DOUGIE   I can't wait 'til you're at my mercy young lady.
          Locked in a hotel room. Who knows what might
          happen?

PETULA   I hope Mr Wobbles isn't threatening me. I might
          not be at home to Mr Wobbles.

DOUGIE   Come here.

          (PETULA *giggles as* DOUGIE *tickles her.* BOB *enters
          holding his head, followed by* MARION.)

BOB   At least he's got the right women this time.

PETULA   Eh?

MARION   Parking meters. Sorry. Round and round in
          circles. Spring up when your back's turned.
          Charge for the air we breath next.

PETULA   Still suffering Bobby? We're lucky. Never get
          hangovers.

MARION   Any sign of Pen-Pen?

BOB   I need some aspirin.

DOUGIE   Place was empty when we came in.

MARION   I'll get you some Bob. Petula. Can you help me
          with the tea things? Battenburg alright? Victoria
          sponges weren't much cop. Scraping of jam and
          all curled up at the edges.

DOUGIE   Fine by me.

PETULA   I'm gasping.

MARION   Probably still dehydrated.

PETULA   (*making face at* DOUGIE) Probably.

          (PETULA *and* MARION *exit.*)

DOUGIE   You ought to try a raw egg, mate. That'd do the
          business. Ever tried that?

(BOB *ignores* DOUGIE.)

DOUGIE   Or half a tin of Andrews shaken up with orange juice.

(BOB *ignores* DOUGIE.)

DOUGIE   Or even a beer mate. Hair of the dog that bit you, eh? No? Oh well. There you go. Just talk to myself for a while, shall I?

BOB   If Petula were in the room I would tell her to tell you that I'm not interested in any of your hangover cures. That my headache will go in its own time. That I'm more than capable of coping on my own thank you.

DOUGIE   Oh right.

BOB   I would also tell her to tell you that at this time I would have more to say to the sofa than I have to say to you.

DOUGIE   Is that so?

BOB   I would tell Petula that I'm quite content to sit here in silence until my wife brings me my tea.

DOUGIE   Fine. Fine. Me too. Wait for tea.

(DOUGIE *sits next to* BOB. DOUGIE *whistles 'Rule Britannia' annoyingly.*)

BOB   If Petula were here I would tell her to tell you to stop whistling that tune which you have whistled non-stop all day even after Marion told you to shut up for whistling it in the middle of Selfridges and making us look like a bunch of morons who'd just stepped off a tour bus!

DOUGIE   Oh come on Bob! Lets call it a day, eh? Eh? Can hardly have an argument through an interpreter when she isn't even in the room.

BOB   I've nothing to say to you.

DOUGIE   Bob. Bobby. I'm sorry. Alright. I stepped over the
             mark. Out of order. Shouldn't have said what I
             said. Eh? Bob?

BOB   You apologise.

DOUGIE   Absobloodylutely mate. And I promise never to
             go to bed with your wife again.

BOB   What?

DOUGIE   Joke mate. Joke. Hey. Come on. Put it there, eh?
             Let's not leave on a sour note. Might be a very
             long time before we meet again. If ever.

             (BOB *shakes* DOUGIE's *hand*.)

BOB   Oh. Oh Alright. Yeah alright you old bastard. Bit
             daft I suppose.

DOUGIE   That's more like it. Here. Not a bad eye you gave
             me. Henry Cooper special.

BOB   Yeah. A corker. Haven't lost my touch. Listen
             I'm . . .

DOUGIE   No worries. All forgotten.

BOB   So. So. I haven't really had a chance to . . . well
             . . . you. You look like you're doing well. How's
             tricks?

DOUGIE   A1 mate. A1. Three day week now. Let the
             workers run the show. Drop in to throw my
             weight around occasionally but my time's my
             own. Spot of golf. Few jars at the club. Top up
             the tan. Best thing I ever did. Make the move. I
             mean Australia was an orchard full of plump
             juicy peaches, ripe for the picking. Pity you
             didn't take me up on my offer. All those years
             ago.

BOB   Ah well. You . . . ssh . . . !

(*Enter* MARION *carrying tray with sandwiches and cake and* PETULA *carrying teapot.*)

MARION   Here we are then. Sandwiches. Hope we're all in favour of salmon paste. Close your eyes and imagine it's the real McCoy. No Petula.

PETULA   Eh?

MARION   On the table thank you.

(PETULA *puts the teapot on the table.*)

PETULA   You boys buried the hatchet?

MARION   Bob. Two paracetamol. Soluble. Give it a twizzle. Sunk to the bottom. A mat. Petula. Don't want a stain.

(MARION *puts mat under teapot.*)

DOUGIE   All pals again aren't we mate?

PETULA   That's a relief. Exhausting doing the talking for two people.

MARION   Bob did you see Pen-Pen this morning?

BOB   My head's exploding.

MARION   No Petula. Let it stand for a while. Well?

BOB   She must have been up with the lark. Could have had three Marion. The dissolving ones are weaker.

PETULA   Well pardon me. Not used to having it stewed.

MARION   Brewed. Not stewed. Brewed. Stop making such a fuss Bob. We're all feeling the after effects.

DOUGIE } I'm not.
PETULA } I'm not.

MARION	Well lucky old you. Must have cast iron constitutions.

(MARION *passes sandwiches around. All eat. They obviously taste horrible.* BOB *takes his apart and inspects it. A silence.*)

MARION	Either eat it or don't eat it. Don't play with it.

PETULA	'Course we don't go much for paste back in Oz. Plenty of fresh fish.

(MARION *stares at* PETULA. *An uncomfortable silence.*)

MARION	I'll go and make some cheese ones.

DOUGIE	Oh no.
PETULA	Don't do that Marion.
BOB	No. It's fine.

PETULA	Alright to have a cup of tea now?

MARION	Yes. Yes!

(MARION *pours tea.*)

BOB	Glad I don't go into town that often. Whole place stinks of hamburgers. Onions and sweat.

PETULA	We enjoyed, Bob.

DOUGIE	Hasn't half changed though. Could do with a spruce up. Dirt. Dossers. Empty offices. Not like I remember.

MARION	Yes. Well. All remember what we want to remember don't we?

DOUGIE	No. It's definitely changed. Like they've all let go. They've all given up.

BOB	Who's they?

DOUGIE	The Brits mate. The Brits.

BOB   What are you talking about. You're a Brit too.

DOUGIE   Not any more mate. Australian and proud.

BOB   Oh for God's sake.

DOUGIE   I'm telling you. Australia's time is only just
            coming.

BOB   Heaven help us.

DOUGIE   Reaching its prime. And the world knows it. Hell.
            We've got the Olympics in the year two thousand.

PETULA   Lovely the boys are talking again isn't it Marion.

DOUGIE   Beat the Poms hands down.

MARION   I'm not so sure Petula.

BOB   You work for the tourist board or something?

DOUGIE   In Australia anyone can make their money and be
            respected for it. None of this old school tie
            business. The class system.

BOB   Ah! Ah! That is where you're wrong!

MARION   Stop shouting Bob. I thought you had a headache.

BOB   We now have a classless society!

MARION   Oh honestly. More tea anyone?

            (MARION *pours more tea.*)

DOUGIE   Oh yeah?

BOB   Yeah. The barriers are being broken down.

MARION   No they're not.

BOB   Shut up Marion.

DOUGIE   Then how come the bulk of your top notch —
            your leading civil servants, your churchmen, your
            lawyers — all went to public school.

BOB   No. No. No. No. You're completely out of touch.

MARION   Leave it Bob.

BOB   Avenues are opening up. Every day of the week.
           Avenues are there for people that weren't there
           before.

MARION   Oh Yes. You can travel up the avenues Bob. Long
           as you can afford the bus fare. If you're in a
           chauffeur driven car all the better. It's the way
           it's always been. Worse in fact.

DOUGIE   There speaks a woman who sees it like it is.

BOB   No. No it's different, it's changing. It's all . . .
           yes . . . it's . . . because . . . because . . . it just is!

MARION   Freshen this up I think. Petula. Should there be
           an encore of last night you'll find the first aid
           box in the hall cupboard.

           (*Exit* MARION *with teapot.*)

BOB   Don't be silly Marion. Here, I'll show you. There
           was . . . yesterday's paper. They interviewed a
           load of . . .

           (BOB *looks inside bottom of display cabinet.*)

PETULA   Still got a queen though haven't you?

BOB   So have you. So have you. You're subjects too.
           Interviewed a cross section. Man in the street sort
           of thing. Usually only get it for the racing.

           (BOB *crosses from display cabinet to bookshelves.
           Notices books out of place.*)

BOB   A typical town. Huntingdon I think. About fifty
           per cent said the barriers had . . . what's this?

DOUGIE   We won't be subjects for much longer. No.
           There's no room for a monarchy in an advanced

society. Ring kissing. Tugging on forelocks. It's feudal, mate. Wake up. New age is dawning. Next century just around the corner. True democracy. That's what we Australians want.

BOB You should be slung in the tower. What's been going on in here — before we came in?

DOUGIE Don't think I should let on — I'm a gentleman.

PETULA Dougie stop it. What do you mean Bob?

BOB The books and that. Looks like a bomb's hit it.

PETULA Like that when we got here. Maybe Pen-Pen's had some friends round.

BOB Marion. Marion!

PETULA A little impromptu party or something.

BOB Pen-Pen doesn't have impromptu parties.

DOUGIE What's up mate?

BOB It's just. It's not right. The lamp. Look at the lamp.

(*A lamp lies on its side.*)

BOB MARION!

(MARION *enters.*)

MARION Alright. Alright. Who's thumped who?

BOB Did you do this?

MARION What? The kettle's boiling.

BOB The books. The lamp.

MARION No. Hadn't noticed to tell the truth. Maybe Dougie and Petula.

DOUGIE Not guilty Marion. Was like that when we came in.

BOB Is anything missing? My cups?

MARION   Oh lord. You don't think . . .

            (BOB *checks his cups.*)

MARION   I'll have a look in the bedroom. Check the rainy
            day tin.

            (*Exit* MARION.)

PETULA   Did I miss something? Why has everyone got ants
            in their pants?

BOB   The front door was locked when you came in.

DOUGIE   Yeah. Had to turn the key.

BOB   And the mortice. Mortice lock was on?

DOUGIE   Now you mention it Bob, no. Just the Yale.

BOB   Always put the mortice on.

PETULA   What about Pen-Pen?

BOB   No. Drummed into her when she was knee-high.
            Let herself in after school. Always the mortice
            on. Second nature.

PETULA   You think someone's been in?

BOB   Ten out of ten Petula.

            (*Enter* MARION.)

MARION   All accounted for.

BOB   The mortice lock was off.

MARION   That's odd. Well. Nothing's gone Bob. Mystery.
            Oh the kettle! Steam'll be taking the wallpaper off.

            (*Exit* MARION. BOB *looks around the room
            puzzled.*)

DOUGIE   Don't worry mate. Sit down. Take the weight off
            your hangover.

PETULA   Ah!

BOB   What?

PETULA   Oh Bobby.

BOB   What. What is it?

PETULA   I don't want you to fly off the handle. I mean
           maybe you moved it. Or Marion did. But. Well.
           What about the stamp collection? Auntie Ruby.

BOB   Oh. Oh. Oh my God. Oh my God. I put it on the . . .

           (BOB *searches the top of the display cabinet
           frantically*.)

BOB   It was there. I know it was. On the top. I m sure I
           . . . unless it's . . .

           (BOB *searches the sideboard and bookshelves*.)

           Marion. Marion. Marion!

DOUGIE   Sure it was there, Bob? We were all a bit far gone
           last night. To be honest I wouldn't have noticed
           if you'd cut it up to make paper chains.

BOB   Could have sworn. Could have sworn.

           (*Enter* MARION *with teapot and another tea-tray*.)

MARION   Made some cheese ones up. I can take a hint.

BOB   Marion!

MARION   I'm right behind you. No need to burst my
           eardrums.

BOB   The stamp collection.

MARION   Stamp collection.

BOB   Yes. Yes. The bloody stamp collection. Did you
           move it?

MARION	The . . . I don't know . . . I . . .
BOB	Think. Think. Last night. I put it on the cabinet. Here. Did you move it?
MARION	Er . . . I . . .
BOB	Marion! THINK!
MARION	I will not be shouted at Bob.
BOB	I'm sorry. But did you? Move it?
MARION	Why would I do that? Oh no. Has it . . . check the sideboard.
BOB	I've done that. I knew this would happen. Just knew it.
MARION	But it was there.
BOB	And lo and bloody behold it isn't there now.
DOUGIE	Don't blow a gasket Bob.
MARION	It must be . . . oh, why us?
BOB	Doesn't take Inspector Morse to work out who's got it.
DOUGIE	Don't jump to conclusions. You suspect foul play call the boys in blue.
BOB	That animal next door, that's who. Probably sitting in there right now. Drooling over a calculator.
MARION	Are we absolutely certain it isn't anywhere else?
BOB	So much for care in the community. I'll give him care in the community across his backside.
PETULA	I think we should all take a deep breath. Relax and think rationally.

BOB   I think you should close your lips . . . shut your
           mouth . . . and keep it shut.

DOUGIE   Eh. Eh. Eh. Eh. Eh. That's my Bubs you're
           talking to.

BOB   It's your Bubs who got us burgled.

DOUGIE   You don't know that.

BOB   I've got a pretty good idea.

MARION   Best call the police I 'spose.

           (MARION *picks up the phone.*)

DOUGIE   I don't see how he got in. Haven't got any keys
           missing, have you?

BOB   Skeleton key. Probably got a pocketful of them.

DOUGIE   Been watching too many movies, mate. It doesn't
           work like that.

BOB   How does it work then Al Capone.

MARION   (*on phone*) Oh. Oh. Yes. Police. Police please.

BOB   All adds up. So and so was walking around doing
           his sums. Put a value on the collection. His
           parting shot was to tell Marion to keep an eye on
           it, the cheeky little . . . I hold you responsible.

DOUGIE   Don't be absurd. How can we be responsible for
           you getting robbed?

BOB   You let him in. It was your idea.

DOUGIE   No it wasn't. It was Petula's.

PETULA   Oh thank you Dougie.

DOUGIE   Hardly her fault if you live in some sort of ghetto.

MARION   (*on phone*) What? Oh. Oh. I see. Right.

BOB   Worth a small fortune. We needed that money.

MARION	We weren't selling it.
BOB	Haven't you got through yet?
MARION	I'm being held in a queue. They're playing a tune. The Blue Danube, I think.
BOB	What? You're what?
PETULA	Let's have a listen.

(PETULA *takes phone from* MARION.)

BOB	This is an emergency. Life or death situation.
MARION	No it isn't.
BOB	Could be though, couldn't it? Could be lying on the floor in a pool of blood while they play music to die to.
MARION	Stop being so dramatic.
PETULA	No. It's definitely a waltz. But it's not the Blue Danube.
DOUGIE	Well I can safely say that this is something that just wouldn't happen in . . .
BOB	Don't say it.
DOUGIE	What.
BOB	Just don't say it.
DOUGIE	Only drawing a parallel mate. There's no way this would happen . . .
BOB	Uh. Uh.
DOUGIE	In Australia.
BOB	How about another shiner? For the sake of symmetry.

DOUGIE   You can't go around bashing people just because
              you disagree with them.

BOB   Give me a better reason.

MARION   Stop it Bob. Calm down.

PETULA   (*on phone*) Oh! Oh hello.

MARION   She's got through.

              (MARION *tries to take phone from* PETULA.)

PETULA   (*on phone*) That was a lovely tune. I wonder if
              you can clear up a little query for me. Now. I
              know it was a waltz but it wasn't the . . . what?

BOB   For God's sake!

PETULA   (*on phone*) No. No. Australia! Yes. That's right.
              Sydney. Oh really? We've got mates up in Perth.
              Yes. Started their own virtual reality arcade. No.
              Did you? Well it's a small old world.

BOB   I don't believe it. I don't bloody believe it. We've
              been robbed and she's doing hands across the sea.

              (BOB *grabs phone from* PETULA.)

              Give that to me.

PETULA   Ouch! No need to be rough Bob. Dougie. Dougie.
              I've split one of my new nails.

BOB   (*on phone*) Is that the police?

DOUGIE   Oh Bubs. Let's have a look.

BOB   (*on phone*) Right. The name's Butler. Bob Butler.
              I'm calling from fifty two . . . what? What?

MARION   I'm sure it'll grow back Petula. They do, you know.

BOB   (*on phone*) A robbery. I want to report a robbery.

PETULA   No Marion. They don't. That's the tragedy. These
            are state of the art silicone.

BOB   (*on phone*) No. No, my flat.

PETULA   Individually tailored and stuck on one by one
            with hypo-allergenic glue. Very exclusive.

BOB   (*on phone*) Burglary then. Alright. Burglary.
            What? No. No listen to me. The next door
            neighbour did it.

MARION   I don't think your silicone fingernails are of the
            utmost importance right now, Petula.

BOB   (*on phone*) I just know. He was here. Last night.
            Eh? Well. He takes medication. Had shifty eyes.
            Definite criminal tendencies.

DOUGIE   Alright to dig into the cake Marion?

MARION   Help yourself Dougie.

            (DOUGIE *pours tea for himself and* PETULA. *They
            dig into the cake*.)

BOB   (*on phone*) Say that again, Sunshine.

PETULA   Lovely young fella that, Marion. Spent last
            summer backpacking around Oz.

BOB   (*on phone*) No you can't bloody talk to the nice
            Australian lady.

DOUGIE   Scored a hit there, Bubs.

BOB   (*on phone*) Do what! I've been robbed and you lot
            sit around on your . . . hello? Hello!

            (BOB *slams phone down*.)

MARION   What happened?

BOB   Phone the local police station he says.
            Undermanned on the switchboard. Doesn't count
            as an emergency.

DOUGIE   Not exactly Brinks Matt is it, mate?

              (DOUGIE, *cake in hand, ambles over to the books.*
              He finds a Wisden's Cricketers Almanac.)

MARION   Phone book, Bob. Dougie you're dropping
              crumbs.

              (BOB *searches through phone book.*)

MARION   Under Police.

DOUGIE   Hey. Hey — look at this!

BOB   I know. I know.

DOUGIE   You got the latest Wisden's. Slaughtered you lot
              in the last series. Have a look at the averages.

BOB   DON'T TOUCH IT!

DOUGIE   Strewth — what?

BOB   Stay where you are. Don't move.

DOUGIE   Blimey — what's the matter?

PETULA   Bobby baby, you're as jumpy as a dingo on heat.

BOB   Fingerprints. They'll want to dust everything
              down.

DOUGIE   Will they?

BOB   Oh yes. I've seen it. On the tele. SOCO. Scene of
              crime officer. They wear white suits and put
              talcum powder on everything.

              (BOB *picks up phone and dials.*)

DOUGIE   Alright to sit down is it?

BOB   Yes. Sit down and shut up.

PETULA   I don't think we need to put up with this
              treatment much longer.

DOUGIE   We won't Bubs. We won't.

PETULA   Not the Bobby I remember. Lost his sense of
            humour. Misery guts.

BOB   I heard that. (*On phone.*) Hello . . . hello.

MARION   Not likely to be the life and soul is he. We've just
            been robbed, for God's sake.

BOB   I . . . words fail me . . . what the . . .

MARION   Is that the police station?

BOB   Yes! Yes I do want to leave a message! This is a
            citizen. A citizen who pays his taxes. Has paid
            his taxes all his working life. A citizen who has
            just been robbed. Will someone please pick up
            this telephone before I throw it out of the
            window. I HAVE BEEN ROBBED! DO YOU
            HEAR ME! I NEED A POLICEMAN! NOW! I
            AM A VICTIM! IS THERE ANYBODY THERE!

            (BOB *slams the phone down.*)

BOB   Damn it Damn it. An answering machine. An
            answering machine. Would you credit it.

MARION   An answering machine. At the police station.

BOB   Some march. The anti-racist shower. Due to
            emergency cover there's no one to take calls. 999
            for life-threatening situations. I ask you. What's
            happening. What is happening.

PETULA   You didn't leave your number.

DOUGIE   Yeah mate. Should have left your number. When
            they've got a spare plod they'll send him round.

BOB   That's it.

MARION   What? That's what?

BOB   That is it. I have had enough. I am taking a stand.

(Exit BOB.*)*

MARION   Bob. Bob. What are you doing?

PETULA   Probably gone to cool off. Here. Have another cuppa. Two sugars. For the shock. We're not unsympathetic Marion. We know what it's like don't we Dougie. We were burgled once.

(PETULA *hands* MARION *cup of tea.*)

MARION   Really. You do get burgled in Australia then. You do surprise me.

PETULA   No need to be sarky Marion.

DOUGIE   Don't think it's as bad as here.

MARION   Couldn't be, could it?

DOUGIE   Only got away with bits and pieces. Ornaments. Some of Petula's jewellery.

PETULA   Costume knick-knacks really. Sort you don't miss. You know.

MARION   No. Not really. I don't. Worry when he's in this sort of mood. Capable of anything. Pressure cooker. Just a matter of time before his lid blows off.

DOUGIE   Found it all two days later of course. Hidden under a pile of barbie bricks on the beach. You can't beat the Sydney police for detection. Kids of course. It's always the kids isn't it?

(BOB *enters. He wears a crash helmet and carries a cricket bat.*)

BOB   Look out world! Here I come!

MARION   Bob. Bob what on earth . . .

BOB   I've had my fill. I'm going in. I'm going to kick
                 some ass!

DOUGIE   Hey Petula. It's Arnold Swarzenegger.

                 (DOUGIE *and* PETULA *laugh.* PETULA *delves into her*
                 bag.)

PETULA   Must get a snap of this.

MARION   Where do you think you're going dressed like
                 that? I hope you don't intend . . .

PETULA   Say cheese!

                 (PETULA *takes flash photograph of* BOB.)

BOB   I'm going next door. I'm going next door to
                 claim my property. And if I don't get satisfaction
                 I'll teach him a lesson. A lesson he'll never
                 forget. Dougie — are you in?

DOUGIE   I would mate. Only I haven't got the hat.

                 (DOUGIE *and* PETULA *laugh.*)

BOB   Fine. Fine. If that's the way it's got to be. Wish
                 me luck Marion.

MARION   No I will not wish you luck. You'll get yourself
                 killed.

BOB   To battle!

                 (*Exit* BOB.)

MARION   Oh my God. Oh my . . . he's doing it. I don't . . .
                 Dougie. Dougie. Stop him!

DOUGIE   I can't stop him. He's made his mind up.

PETULA   You stay where you are Bubs.

MARION   Someone's got to do something.

DOUGIE   He'll soon change his mind when he gets to the
          door and remembers how big he is.

MARION   Damn you both.

PETULA   Marion.

          (MARION *makes for the door.* DOUGIE *blocks her
          way.*)

DOUGIE   Hey. Hey. Hey. Where do you think you're going?

MARION   Might as well make it a double suicide.

DOUGIE   Alright. You stay here. Though Lord knows why
          I'm doing this.

MARION   You're supposed to be his friend. Ran away and
          left him to it all those years ago. Make amends
          why don't you.

          (*Exit* DOUGIE. MARION *searches for* BOB'S
          cigarettes and lights up.)

PETULA   Marion! You're smoking.

MARION   Oh well done.

PETULA   But I thought you'd given up. What about your
          health? Cancer and all that. And it's terrible for
          the skin. Makes your face dry up. Give you
          appalling lines sweetheart.

MARION   Good. Good. Hope I end up with a face like a
          rhinos' arse!

PETULA   What! You don't mean that. Now you listen to me
          Marion . . .

MARION   No. No. You listen to me. And listen to me hard.
          Just don't get it Petula do you? All washes over.
          Pours off your back like one of your oh so
          exclusive beauty treatments. Couldn't see the
          nose in front of your face when you were
          nineteen. May have contact lenses now but you're

just as short-sighted. Things have changed. Once
upon a time this was the land of knees-ups in the
boozer. Three Baccardis and a pickled egg then
round to a neighbours for a late night snifter.
Doors open. Doors always open. Men worked
together. Kids played together. Mothers gossiped
together. Little Tommy rushed to hospital with a
septic boil and old Mother Brown in number forty
two knew about it before his dad. It's a postcard,
Petula. One of those sepia photographs with 'Old
England' written underneath. It's finished. Gone.
Once upon a time there were comic book
gangsters in sharp suits with family ties. Honour
among thieves. Saw you alright because your
uncle had a stall next to their uncle in the
market. Robbing the rich to feed the poor. Now
it's the poor who get robbed. At knife point.
Thugs with portable phones and diamonds in
their teeth. Pensioners mugged for the milk
money. Guns. Drugs. Stranger steps into the lift
and you're checking the keys in your pocket to
see if they'll make a weapon. Fear. Kids hanging
around. No dole 'til they're eighteen. No jobs.
Growing up in these hutches. What are they
going to do? Become missionaries? Starve a dog
for too long and it'll turn on you. And it's
turning. Slowly. Ready to sink its teeth into any
scapegoat. Bully boys on street corners. Shoving
their so-called literature into your hand. Winning
votes. Gaining confidence. So please, Petula.
Don't lecture me about smoking. Cancer? I'm
living in a cancer. This is 1994. The Pearly King
and Queen have shut up shop and moved into
sheltered housing because they can't take having
petrol poured through their letter box any more.

(PETULA *is shocked into silence.*)

MARION   Here. Another slice of Battenburg.

(MARION *puts piece of cake on plate and gives it
to* PETULA.)

PETULA   Obviously needed to get that off your chest.

MARION	Oh I did Petula. I did.
PETULA	Shame you didn't get out when you had the chance.
MARION	What chance? What do you mean?
PETULA	Thought it didn't add up. You really are in the dark aren't you? I don't think Bobby's been entirely honest with you.
MARION	Spit it out Petula. Whatever it is.
PETULA	All supposed to be a big secret of course. Dougie hasn't got an inkling that I know. But it's wise for a wife to keep an eye on her husband's filing cabinet don't you think?
MARION	What are you driving at?
PETULA	Bear with me Marion. Bear with me. About five years after we made the move. Dougie was working for this bloke. Geoff Bacon. Bit of a playboy. Hooked to the pokies. You know — slot machines. Had some Sheila in Singapore. On the side of course. Wifey didn't have a notion. Anyway. He went on the diddle. Filching from the company to pay for the air fares. Authorities were on to him. Not keeping proper accounts. All that jazz. So. Dougie bailed him out. Raised a loan. Put in an offer for the company. Knock down price of course. But poor old Bacon had to accept. Ended up with a cap in front of him playing accordion by the harbour.
MARION	Where's all this leading, Petula?
PETULA	Soon after. Videos taking off like nobody's business. Raking it in we were. Dougie had a big plan for expansion. Built a new workshop. Took on extra workers. And that's when he wrote to Bob. He wrote to Bob and asked him to come over and manage for him.
MARION	What?

PETULA   Was going to pay top whack. Plane tickets. Set up
           a cheap mortgage. The works. Even school fees
           for Pen-Pen. Great opportunity.

MARION   But he never even mentioned it to me.

PETULA   Really? Now that is interesting. Because Bob
           painted a different picture. In his letters. There
           was quite a bundle. Dougie really wanted him.
           Thanks for the offer, he said. But Marion's tied
           to the old country. Marion doesn't want to move.

MARION   I can't believe he did that. I'll kill him.

PETULA   And there was me thinking you'd made a choice.
           I do hope I haven't opened up a can of worms.
           That would be a shame.

           (*Enter* BOB *and* DOUGIE.)

BOB   We're back! We're back! Marion. Should have
           seen me in action, eh Dougie?

DOUGIE   It was quite something, Bob.

BOB   Nailed him to the wall. Thrown the book at him.
           Justice has been done.

DOUGIE   Wasn't exactly trial by jury, was it mate?

BOB   Knocked on the door. Poised I was. Like this.
           With my bat. So he knows I mean business.
           Opens up slowly. You! I said. You! I've got a
           bone to pick with you. Let me in! Didn't know
           what to make of me.

DOUGIE   Think he realised you weren't suggesting a quick
           innings before sundown.

BOB   Marched into the living room. Pointed at his dog.
           Told him to lock it in the kitchen. And he did.

DOUGIE   You would, wouldn't you. With a cricket hat
           hovering over your head.

BOB | An Aladdin's cave in there, Marion. Enough electrical goods to drain the National Grid. Worth thousands. Like to know where you got this little lot from I said.

DOUGIE | Hi-fi fan. His redundancy money.

BOB | That's his story. So. I said I believe you have something that belongs to me. What, he says. Butter wouldn't melt. What? I said I don't play games with me, sunny Jim and I swung like this a couple of times. To show how I meant business.

(BOB *demonstrates with his cricket bat.*)

DOUGIE | Smashed the light fitting.

BOB | Haven't got anything he says. And I walked up to him and looked him straight in the eye.

DOUGIE | The nose Bob. The nose. He's a lot taller than you.

BOB | And I whispered. Threateningly. Where is it?

DOUGIE | Just like Larry Olivier in the Marathon Man.

BOB | Don't know what you're talking about, he says. I said give it back right now or I'll take a swipe at your fancy TV set. And he shakes his head. And crash! Crash! I brought my bat down.

DOUGIE | Through the screen. Sparks flying. Lucky you didn't get a shock, mate.

BOB | I was the one doling out the shocks. I turned to him and I said maybe that's loosened your tongue. Thought that was good. Loosened your tongue.

DOUGIE | Very Dirty Harry.

BOB | And he's looking scared, really scared. Want to tell me where it is, I said. No reply. And crash! Onto his video. Broke it up. Completely. Last chance, I said. Last chance or the stereo goes.

DOUGIE   Top of the range, Bang and Olufson.

BOB   Why are you doing this, he says and I counted to
              three.

DOUGIE   Just for effect.

BOB   Just for effect. He keeps stum. Standing there
              with his mouth open. And. Crash! Did his hi-fi in
              and all. Picked up my bat. Slung it over my
              shoulder. And walked out. Cool as a cucumber.

PETULA   What about the collection Bob?

BOB   Eh?

PETULA   The stamp collection. He gave it back to you.

BOB   Er. No. No, he didn't. But hell. It didn't half feel
              good. Come on then Marion. How about a kiss for
              the champion?

              (BOB *takes off his crash helmet and proffers his
              cheek.* MARION *walks up to him slowly then
              smacks him hard on the face.*)

PETULA   Marion!

BOB   What did you do that for?

MARION   I want a kidney-shaped swimming pool.

BOB   I want an MG Magnet but slapping you around
              the face isn't going to get me one.

DOUGIE   What's going on — Petula?

MARION   I want to have barbecues and go sheep shearing.

BOB   What?

MARION   I want to wear purple and orange swimsuits and
              pick fresh fruit from trees in the garden.

BOB   What are you talking about?

MARION   I want to go scuba diving and explore the Great
                Barrier Reef.

BOB   You can't swim. Have you been drinking? Have
                you? I see. While I was next door risking life and
                limb you've been sitting in here knocking them
                back. Any opportunity.

MARION   Oh yes. I'll take any opportunity. Like the
                opportunity to go to Australia. Ring a bell does
                it? The opportunity to be with Auntie Ruby. The
                opportunity to get away from this bloody awful
                place. The opportunity that presented itself all
                those years ago that you didn't even bother to tell
                me about. How dare you Bob. How dare you. You
                even told him it was because of me we couldn't go.

BOB   Whoops.

MARION   Yes. Whoops Bob. Whoops.

BOB   (*to* PETULA) You told Marion about Dougie's little
                plan.

DOUGIE   Petula.

PETULA   Slipped out, Bubs. I thought she knew. I thought
                it was Marion who threw the spanner in the
                works.

MARION   Little plan. I'll give you little plan. That little
                plan would've saved out lives. Just because it was
                Dougie making the offer. You and your pride
                Bob. It'll be the death of me.

                (*Sound of video entry buzzing.*)

BOB   It was the wrong time love.

PETULA   Is that the video entry?

BOB   Didn't want to worry you. Depressed you were.
             On the happy pills.

PETULA   Is someone going to get that?

MARION   Is it any wonder I was on the bloody happy pills.
             Cooped up in a tower block with a screaming kid.

PETULA   Still buzzing. I think you ought to answer it.

MARION   If you're that worried why don't you get off your
             designer clad bum and answer it yourself!

PETULA   Well. I've never heard the like.

MARION   You may be many things Bob. But I never had
             you down as a liar.

             (*Exit* MARION.)

PETULA   Right. All packed next door. Just have to pop our
             coats on.

BOB   Well thanks a bunch Petula. Can't resist can you?
             Had to stick the knife in.

DOUGIE   There was no need to drag all that up, Bubs.

PETULA   She was having a go at me. Moaning about how
             hard done by she was. Set the record straight
             that's all.

DOUGIE   Been snooping through my private papers again
             haven't you sweetheart?

BOB   As if I didn't have enough on my plate. Can live
             without having arguments about something that
             happened ten years ago.

DOUGIE   You were happy to dig up the dirt last night.

BOB   She need never have known. Ignorance is bliss
             and all that.

PETULA   You haven't a leg to stand on Bob, so you can
          stop laying the blame at my doorstep. It's your
          funeral.

BOB   You can say that again.

          (*Enter* MARION.)

MARION   Wanted a policeman, didn't you Bob?

BOB   What. Yeah.

MARION   Well your boat's come in. There's two of them
          downstairs. With your daughter. She's been
          arrested.

BOB   She's been what?

MARION   They're bringing her up in the lift.

          (*Exit* MARION.)

DOUGIE   Like father like daughter, eh?

BOB   You . . . don't push me.

          (*Exit* BOB.)

PETULA   Thank you for your loyalty.

DOUGIE   All I said was I thought there was no need . . .

          (PETULA *gathers up her belongings frenetically.*)

PETULA   We are going. Going. Don't touch me. I shall
          remain composed while we make our excuses. But
          that's it. Do you hear me? Nightmare from start
          to finish. Fights. Slanging matches. Thought
          we'd have some peace once you two had made up.
          But oh no. Bob's turned into the Incredible Hulk
          with a bellyful of grudges. I've taken more insults
          in the last half hour than I've had in a lifetime.
          My nerves are shot to pieces. If I were in this
          state back home Monica would immediately

suggest double sessions. I'd be spending every
waking moment in the lotus position.

DOUGIE   Eh. Eh. Eh. Don't fly off the handle. We can't
just storm off. Their kid's in trouble.

PETULA   It's all very well spinning daydreams on a lilo.
Sinking Pina Coladas by the pool and taking a
squiffy stroll down memory lane. Reality is a
different kettle of fish. It's slushy thinking that
brought us here. Next time it's a hotel.

DOUGIE   Ok. Ok. Just keep your voice down.

PETULA   Sleeping in a teenager's bedroom. That hairy ape
with his hand on his crotch staring down at us
from the wall. Not even enough room to hang my
clothes. This place is a dump!

DOUGIE   Petula.

PETULA   And no more letters. We become incommunicado.
No postcards. Notice they haven't got any pinned
up? That's how much we're appreciated. And no
parcels at Christmas. No more keeping up
connections. The correspondence stops now.

DOUGIE   Whatever you say sweetheart.

PETULA   You walking around with your tongue hanging
out. Flirting with Marion like there's no
tomorrow.

DOUGIE   When?

PETULA   Just now. All gooey and slimy. Practically left a
trail on the floor. Lord knows what you see in her.

DOUGIE   I . . . I don't . . . I didn't see anything.

PETULA   Didn't you. Must have been temporary blindness
brought on by an overload of testosterone.

DOUGIE   Imagining things.

PETULA   It's a pity you didn't sleep together all those years ago. Maybe then you'd have got it out of your system.

DOUGIE   Here. Let me give you a hand. Sweetheart.

(*Enter* MARION, BOB *and* PEN *clutching a bag of sweets with a rucksack on her back.*)

PEN   Kangaroos are still here then.

DOUGIE   Pen-Pen. How's it going, mate?

PEN   Thought you'd have had enough by now.

DOUGIE   What happen? They catch you pinching sweets or something?

(BOB *paces up and down, agitated.*)

PEN   Policeman gave them to me. Think he thought I was going to throw up in the car.

PETULA   The car?

DOUGIE   Where've you been kiddo?

PEN   Nowhere.

BOB   What?

MARION   Bob.

BOB   Nowhere? Nowhere? Don't give me your nowheres my girl. You've been somewhere alright. Picked up at the airport with two thousand pounds in her pocket.

PETULA   Strewth.

DOUGIE   The airport. What were you doing there?

MARION   Oh boy.

BOB   Hand it over. Come on.

PEN   What?

BOB   The passport.

            (PEN *opens her rucksack, finds passport and
            hands it to* BOB.)

BOB   You don't get this back in a hurry. Half a day's
            wages this cost me. Wondered why you wanted
            one. You must think I'm soft. Don't need a
            passport to cross the channel. Oh no. But I want
            one she says. So I've got some ID.

PEN   That's true.

BOB   Ferry trips across the channel. You had no
            intention of crossing the channel.

PEN   I did. You weren't going to let me.

BOB   Funny sort of ferry that runs out of Heathrow
            airport.

PEN   I didn't . . .

BOB   Or has there been some major canal building
            going on that I just haven't heard about?

PEN   Don't be stupid.

BOB   There's going to be a change of tune. Oh yes. I'm
            going to frog march you down to that Job Centre
            every morning.

PEN   But there's nothing . . .

BOB   I want you working. I want you so dog tired you
            haven't got the energy to give me and your
            mother the runaround. And I want an
            explanation. And I want it now.

PEN   I haven't got an explanation.

BOB   Think of one. Fast.

            (BOB *advances on* PEN. MARION *blocks his way.*)

PETULA   Bobby. Marion. We'll say adios. Holiday to be
            getting on with. Train to catch.

MARION   Stay Petula. What's a bit more dirty washing
            between friends.

BOB   Should sling you out once and for all.

PEN   Why don't you then. Go on.

MARION   This isn't getting us anywhere.

DOUGIE   Great rucksack you've got there Pen-Pen. All
            kitted up for some serious backpacking.

BOB   Shut up Dougie.

PEN   Didn't get very far did I?

DOUGIE   Hang on a moment.

MARION   Yes. Shut up Dougie.

PETULA   I'm sorry but I really don't think this is any way
            to treat a child.

BOB   You wouldn't last more than two minutes on the
            street.

MARION   Oh really. And what do you know about raising
            children, Petula?

PEN   It'd feel more like home.

PETULA   I know that a kind word goes a long way.
            Children are like current accounts. You get out
            what you put in.

BOB   Like that would you? A sleeping bag on the
           embankment? With the winos and the pimps.

MARION   I am not going to stand here and take childcare
           advice from a woman with blocked tubes!

PETULA   What! What! Dougie. Dougie. How could you!

PEN   Only reason you want me here is so I can skivvy
           for you. Extra pair of hands. Useful for the
           shopping and the washing up.

DOUGIE   Eh. Eh. Bubs. Don't get upset. Please. Marion —
           that was uncalled for.

PETULA   Bastard Dougie. I . . . what other little secrets
           have you been sharing with Marion?

BOB   You are an ungrateful brat!

PEN   You won't even hear me out.

PETULA   Why not shout it from the rooftops. Petula can't
           have children — nothing to do with me!

DOUGIE   It slipped out. I'm sorry. Supposed to be in
           confidence. Sweetheart, come on.

BOB   Got all the answers haven't you. Backchat. All I
           get from you.

PEN   Supposed to just shut up and take it am I. Not
           allowed a fair hearing.

PETULA   What else have you been blabbing about. Tell me
           Dougie out with it. Behind my back. Marion — of
           all people.

MARION   I am going to explode. I swear. I'm exploding.

DOUGIE   There's no point shouting at me. None. It's true
           isn't it? I'm sorry love but it's true.

BOB   Oh, just push off. Go on. Push off!

PETULA	True maybe, but I don't want my gynaecological problems broadcast. Can't trust you as far as I can . . . Don't expect a kind word from me for a very long time.
DOUGIE	If I can't have a talk with a very old friend. You're overreacting. Doesn't matter — do you hear me — there is no need for a row.
PEN	Fine. Fine. Then I'll go.
MARION	I can't bear this. I cannot bear this.
BOB	And don't think you can come running back here when you're starving with no shoes on your feet.

PEN   I'll leave a note in my pocket. If they find my body they'll know who to sting for the funeral expenses.

(PEN *makes to go.* MARION *dashes onto the balcony.*)

MARION   SHUT UP! EVERYONE. RIGHT NOW. OR I SWEAR I SHALL JUMP OFF THE BALCONY!

(*Everyone is shocked into silence.* MARION *grabs* PEN *and pushes her into a chair.*)

MARION   You . . . Sit . . . Not . . . A . . . Word.

(MARION *pushes* BOB *into a chair.*)

MARION   Here. Have a fag. Nice and relaxed. Nice and calm. Drink. Come on, have a drink.

(MARION *puts cigarette in* BOB's *mouth and lights it. Picks up can of beer from sideboard, opens it and puts it in* BOB's *hand.*)

MARION   Dougie. Can't stand there empty-handed.

(MARION *opens another can and hands it to* DOUGIE.)

DOUGIE   I'm not really in the . . .

MARION   Drink it. Now.

DOUGIE   Yes Marion.

MARION   Petula. An eggnog. A nice glass of eggnog. Bit of
            nutrition with your alcohol.

            (MARION *pours large glass of eggnog and hands it
            to* PETULA.)

PETULA   I'm not a great fan of . . .

MARION   Not — A — Word.

            (PETULA, DOUGIE, BOB *and* PEN *are cowed into
            submission.* MARION *pours herself an eggnog.*)

MARION   Lovely. Lovely. Lovely. Everyone happy? Good.
            That's good. Pen-Pen. You have our complete
            attention. Absolute silence. You will tell us all
            exactly what happened in your own time. In your
            own words. Bob. One grunt from you and I will
            smash you over the head with your cricket bat.
            Dougie. So much as a murmur about the
            wonderful land of Oz and I will pour that beer
            down your very expensive shirt. And Petula. One
            squeak from your very own version of Doctor
            Spock and I will snap off your priceless
            fingernails one by one. Is that understood?

            (*Silence.*)

MARION   Good. Pen-Pen.

PEN   I . . . I don't know . . . I mean. I. Hard to . . . I
            don't know where to start.

MARION   From the beginning.

PEN   Last night. You were all in bed. I was sitting in
            here. Couldn't sleep. Tried . . . but. Just sitting.
            Listening to the traffic. Not thinking about
            anything. Drifting. Staring into space. And then.

This cloud came down. We get low cloud
sometimes — we're that high up. You can walk
out onto the balcony and stand in it. Stand in a
cloud. Feel the wet on your cheeks. You can't see
three feet in front of you. I stood there for ages.
Looking into the whiteness and wondered where
it came from. The cloud. I saw a programme once
— how it works you know. Thought maybe it had
come from the mountains. The Cotswolds. Or
France — over the channel. But then I thought
no. No more likely the Thames. Tiny drops of
water sucked up from that big brown snake over
there. Dirty. Stale. And . . . well. It was . . . just
like that. Right then. That I made up my mind.
To go. Got my stuff together — not much. Couple
of pairs of jeans. T-shirts. That jumper you
knitted me with the baggy collar and the dinosaur
on the front. Sneaked into the kitchen and filled
up an empty ice cream box with your cheese
straws, Mum. In case I was hungry. And then I . .
. I'm sorry Mum. I am. I know I . . . but I saw it
and . . . I knocked the lamp over. Messed the
books up so you'd think maybe . . . but . . . well .
. . before I knew it I'd stuffed it into my
rucksack. The stamp collection.

(BOB *makes to interrupt.* MARION *stops him.*)

I didn't know where I was going. Just that I was.
Going, I mean. Kept repeating it. Over and over.
In my head. I'm going. I'm going. Walked into
town. Through the City. Shift workers and
cleaners pouring out of basements. Night people.
Grey. Like mice. I'm going. I'm going I thought.
It was an old-fashioned shop just off St Martin's
Lane. Stained glass in the window. Big brass
sign. 'Commemorative Issues and First Day
Covers Bought and Sold'. Pressed my face
against the shop front to see what was inside.
Man came out. Brown overall. Holes in the
pockets. Smelled of dust and glue. So . . . I . . . I
took it out. I showed it to him. Found the Penny
Blue and he got excited. Foot tapping on the
floor. Little glints of sweat mixed in with the

dandruff in his eyebrows. Two thousand he said.
The lot. Two thousand. Cash. In cash. I did try.
To argue. Remembered him saying the Penny
Blue was worth five. That it was rare. Valuable.
But. Must have looked too keen to sell. Took me
out the back. Old safe with a handle on the front.
Opened it up and gave me the money. He was
really sweaty by then. Splashes of salt water
falling onto the notes. Coughed into his sleeve
and reached out. He tried to touch my hair. I ran.
I knew it was wrong Mum, I did. I knew . . . but
. . . it was like being pushed and this thing in my
head on and on, I'm going, I'm going. Down the
tube. Slipped on a pizza box. Nearly dropped the
money. Pushed it into my waistband envelope
scratching my stomach. I took the train. It was
there. I didn't realise. I didn't. I didn't know.
Honest. But it was going . . . going to the airport.
I stood in front of the board. The board that
makes clicking noises when it turns over. Saw all
the places. Amazing places. Advert places. Felt
the money. Still there. And I thought. I can go. If
I want to. Passport's in my bag. I can go. So I
will. And that's when I decided. Australia. I was
going to Australia. Went to the loo. Drank some
water from the tap. Disgusting. There was lady.
Flowers in her hand. She saw me. Her son. He
was going. Going for good. His choice, she said.
His life. Had to keep her chin up. She tried to put
mascara on but it slid about. Black zigzags down
her cheek. Thought I'm glad there's no one
crying for me. Making a mess. Lady at the ticket
desk looked like a model in a poster. Long blonde
hair. Teeth like snow. One way ticket I said.
Sydney please. Pay in cash thank you very much.
She asked for my passport. Told me to sit down.
Had to make a phone call, she said. I felt a bit
sad then. Mum. But I'd gone too far. Couldn't
stop. I was going. I was definitely going. I
thought it was best. Just to disappear. No note.
No calls. No nothing. Just go missing and start
again. Somewhere fresh. Tapped me on the
shoulder. Two coppers. Where did I get the
money from. Mind your own I said. Told me you

had to have a visa. Where's my visa. Didn't know
that. I didn't know that Mum. Brought me back.
Back here. Well . . . here I am. You heard them.
Up to you. Can press charges if you want. I'm
back. But . . . I . . . I had to go. Had to go Mum.
I'm sorry. Really . . . but . . . it was just . . .
standing out there. Last night. In that cloud. And
thinking. Thinking I wanted to be somewhere
else. That's all. In a different cloud. You know?
Mum. Mum. Do you understand?

MARION   Yes. Yes I do Pen-Pen. Wish I didn't. But I do.

BOB   Australia.

DOUGIE   Kiddo. If we'd known you'd wanted to go to Oz . . .

BOB   Of all places.

PETULA   Dougie.

DOUGIE   So bad. I mean. We would have sorted you out.

PETULA   Sweetheart.

BOB   Two thousand pounds in your pocket and pick
            Australia.

DOUGIE   Seen you alright for a trip over, eh Bubs?

PETULA   Well. Possibly. We should be thinking about . . .

BOB   You must be dafter than I thought.

DOUGIE   Anytime love. Drop us a line.

PETULA   In a year or two maybe.

BOB   No chance of that.

DOUGIE   Bubs!

BOB   No chance at all.

PETULA   Haven't got the space Dougie. Once the
            extension's built. Maybe. But. Have a think about
            alternative arrangements Pen-Pen.

PEN   Enjoy sleeping in my room did you?

PETULA   I shall ignore that.

BOB   Be lucky if you make it as far as the corner shop.

DOUGIE   Come on Bob. The kid's miserable.

PETULA   Leave it Dougie. It's a domestic. Don't stick your
          oar in. It won't be appreciated.

DOUGIE   Can you blame her?

PETULA   Look we'd better . . .

MARION   You're heading off then.

DOUGIE   Oh. Right. Yeah.

PETULA   Thank you for having us.

DOUGIE   Cheers and all that. Then. Hit the road. Take care
          me old china. Thanks for everything. And . . .
          well. All come out in the wash, eh?

BOB   Yeah. Yeah. Cheers Dougie. Have a safe trip.

MARION   I'll see you out.

PETULA   Dougie. Come on.

DOUGIE   No worries. Bags are in the hallway. See you kid.
          Don't let the bastards grind you down, eh?

          (*Exit* DOUGIE *and* PETULA.)

BOB   Hear that? Can you hear that? They're at it again.
          Scratching about. Must be dozens of them —
          listen to it.

          (BOB *unscrews the cover from the heating grill.*)

MARION   What were you thinking of Pen-Pen?

PEN   I know . . . I know. I'm sorry. I know it was the
          last bit of Auntie Ruby and that. I didn't think . . .

MARION   That doesn't matter, do you hear me? As long as
              you're here. In one piece. Don't do anything like
              that again. Just. Just. Just to go. Just to
              disappear. What do you think that would have
              been like? Seeing your empty room every day.
              Wondering if you were sitting somewhere with a
              needle in your arm. Or roaming the streets with
              some pimp chasing you. Or . . . or lying in a
              ditch. How do you think we could have lived with
              that?

PEN   Didn't think you'd care.

              (BOB *takes his shoe off and holds it above his
              head.*)

MARION   Of course we'd care. We do care. You silly girl.
              I've got work tonight but later. Later we'll sort
              this out. Properly. Once and for all.

              (BOB *thrashes at something inside the heating
              grill.*)

BOB   Damn it.

MARION   That's right Bob. Rome is burning and you play
              catch the cockroach.

PETULA   (off) AAAAAAAAAAAAAAAAAAAAAAAAAH!

              (BOB *leaps up.*)

BOB   What the . . . What was that?

MARION   Sounded like Petula. Thought we'd seen the back
              of them.

BOB   What's she screaming for?

              (MARION *makes her way towards the exit just as*
              PETULA *appears walking strangely.* DOUGIE *follows
              behind her.*)

PETULA   Oh my God. Oh my God. Dougie. Dougie. Are
            you there?

DOUGIE   Right behind you sweetheart. Keep going. Keep
            going.

            (TREVOR *appears holding a shotgun. Carrying a
            black bin liner.*)

MARION   Bob! Bob — he's got a — do something.

            (TREVOR *jumps onto table.*)

TREVOR   My turn to bat I think. Old chap. Only I haven't
            got the equipment. Have to use a gun. Play my
            way now.

DOUGIE   Not what I call cricket mate.

BOB   What are . . . what are you doing?

TREVOR   Fighting. Fighting fire with fire.

BOB   Listen I . . . I. Lot of strain. Lot of strain recently
            and . . .

TREVOR   DON'T MOVE!

BOB   Don't shoot! Not moving. Not moving. No. No.
            Look. It's. It's all a big. An enormous. Mistake
            mate. Yes? Not you. Not your . . . oh no. Not
            guilty. Innocent. Pure as the driven. Oh Lord.
            Lord . . . sorry?

MARION   I don't think that's going to do it Bob.

TREVOR   You!

PEN   Me?

TREVOR   Fill it up.

            (TREVOR *passes* PEN *the bin liner.*)

PETULA   We're going to die. We are going to die.

TREVOR   Cups. Put the cups in.

(PEN *puts cups from display cabinet into bin liner*.)

PETULA   WE'RE GOING TO DIE. WE'RE GOING TO DIE!

MARION   Shut up Petula.

BOB   Keep a couple back, eh?

TREVOR   All of them.

BOB   Not the pop-quiz shield. I actually won that one.

TREVOR   I said all of them. Put it in.

           (PEN *puts shield into bin liner*.)

PETULA   We'll be on the news. In the papers.

TREVOR   The CD. The CD Walkman.

           (PEN *opens her rucksack. Takes out the CD Walkman and puts it in the bin liner*.)

PETULA   Carnage in a council flat. That's what they'll say. Slaughter on the fourteenth floor. Genocide in the clouds.

DOUGIE   Petula! Will you shut up!

TREVOR   Watches. Jewellery.

           (*All take off their watches and rings as* PEN *passes round the bin liner*.)

BOB   It's only a Casio. Free with ten litres of Two Star. Not worth . . .

TREVOR   Hand it over.

BOB   Yes. Yes. Done.

PETULA   Can't get at it Dougie. My butterfly's all stuck up at the back.

DOUGIE   Here. Here.

(PETULA *struggles with her earring.* DOUGIE *helps her.*)

DOUGIE   Won't budge. Jammed rigid. I think you've had that mate.

TREVOR   That's alright.

PETULA   Oh good.

TREVOR   Not a problem.

PETULA   Thank God for that.

TREVOR   Just have to chop your ear off.

PETULA   What! Dougie — Dougie!

(DOUGIE *yanks on* PETULA'S *ear and detaches earring.*)

PETULA   Ouch!

DOUGIE   Got it.

TREVOR   Bring it here.

(PEN *gives bin liner to* TREVOR.)

TREVOR   Oh dear. Oh dear. Oh dear.

BOB   What? What's the matter?

TREVOR   You're on a sticky wicket, mate.

BOB   Oh yes.

TREVOR   I've got a bit of a problem.

MARION   Really Trevor. You do surprise me.

(TREVOR *sorts through spoils in bin liner.*)

TREVOR   See. In our first match. Daddy over there. Daddy caused a bit of damage. Very impressive. Human bomb. But it leaves me with a headache. This little lot. Peanuts. No. No way. Just not going to do it. Nowhere near. What am I going to do about that then?

(TREVOR *raises his shotgun at* BOB.)

BOB	No. No. We can work this out. Oh yes. I'm sure we can. Let's be civilised.
DOUGIE	Stuff civilised. Wonga mate.
BOB	What?
DOUGIE	Wonga. Wonga!
BOB	Wonga wonga to you and all.
DOUGIE	Pretty green. Folding paper. Dosh. Money. Give him some money you moron.
BOB	Eh? Oh.
MARION	Pen-Pen. The money. The stamp money. Quickly.

(PEN *looks in her rucksack.*)

PETULA	Dougie. I've changed my mind. I want to be cremated.
MARION	Hurry Pen-Pen.
DOUGIE	Not now, Bubs. Not now.
PEN	Put it at the bottom. Keep it safe.
PETULA	Cremated and scattered downwind of the Opera House.
DOUGIE	For God's sake!
PEN	Found it.
MARION	Give it to your father.

(PEN *gives money to* BOB.)

PETULA	Then all the gang back to the house for a barbie. Open that anniversary Jeroboam. Seafood and a selection of . . .

DOUGIE	Petula! One goes we all go. I won't be around to uncork bubbly and put up streamers at your bloody funeral party. Now shut up!
BOB	Here. Here. Look at this. Two thousand pounds.
PEN	One thousand nine hundred and ninety five.
BOB	What. Oh.

(BOB *digs into his pocket and finds a five-pound note.*)

PEN	Bought a magazine.
BOB	There. A fiver. Two thousand, eh. Cover the damage. Yes. Yes. No harm done.

(TREVOR *takes the money. He keeps the gun pointed at* BOB.)

DOUGIE	Come on mate. Fair's fair. He's given you the money. Put the gun down.

(TREVOR *steps off the table and advances on* BOB.)

TREVOR	Yeah I've got the money. But what about my dog?
BOB	Your dog? What about your dog?
TREVOR	He's all upset. Doesn't like loud noises.
BOB	Sorry. Sorry to hear that.
TREVOR	Wouldn't eat his Pedigree Chum.
BOB	Have you tried Winnelot?
PETULA	Hail Mary full of grace . . .
MARION	Stop it Petula.
TREVOR	And when my dog's upset . . . I'm upset.
PETULA	Hail Mary . . .

MARION Shut up — you're not even a Catholic. He'll give you anything you want Trevor. Just ask. Anything.

TREVOR Anything.

BOB Anything at all. Your wish is my command. Just fire away!

MARION No! Don't!

TREVOR Don't know. Don't know if I want anything. Just so pent up. You know. Can't help myself. Getting upset. Boosts my adrenalin. Sends my chemicals haywire. Medication stops working.

PETULA Have you tried Yoga? Very good for stress.

DOUGIE Petula. Will you shut up. Or do I have to make you.

PETULA Dougie!

(TREVOR *advances on* BOB *and takes aim.*)

TREVOR Get down. Go on. On your knees.

(BOB *falls to his knees.*)

BOB Oh God. Oh God. Another thousand. Eh? Another thousand. Should just about . . . if we . . . we write you a cheque. Yes. Write you a cheque right now . . . or . . . a car! Yes! How about a car? Nice shiny souped up number, eh? From the workshop. Please. Please don't shoot. A car. A car. I'll get you a bloody car.

TREVOR No. No. It won't do. Bob. Time you were bowled out I think.

(TREVOR *cocks his shotgun.*)

BOB   Noooooooooooooooooooooooo!
MARION Oh my Gooooooooooooooooooooo!
PETULA Aaaaaaaaaaaaaaaaaaaaaaaaaaaa!
DOUGIE Don't shoooooooooooooooooooooooooo!
PEN   Daaaaaaaaaaaaaaaaaaaaaaaaaaaaa!

(TREVOR *pulls the trigger. A bunch of flowers appears from the end of the barrel. A silence.* TREVOR *laughs. Then stops suddenly.*)

TREVOR   Owzat!

BOB   Jesus. Jesus Christ.

              (MARION *tends to* BOB.)

MARION   Bob. Bob. My God. Are you alright? You're shaking.

BOB   Ha. Very good. Very good. Had me going for a minute there mate. Well done.

TREVOR   Sussed.

              (TREVOR *picks up the bin liner.*)

TREVOR   Thanks for the compensation.

BOB   Oh don't mention it.

TREVOR   Found what you were looking for then?

BOB   Yes. Er. Yes. Pen-Pen. Misunderstanding.

TREVOR   Sweet. You're learning kid.

              (TREVOR *makes towards exit.*)

              I'll drop by. Mates now. Have another drink. Neighbours. Everybody needs good neighbours. Eh? Be in touch anyway. About the car.

BOB   Eh?

TREVOR   The one you promised me. (*To* DOUGIE.) Want to watch her. Bit of a goer with a microphone in her hand.

PETULA   Oh honestly.

TREVOR   (*to* PEN) Rock on sister. Rock on.

              (*Exit* TREVOR.)

PETULA   (*in tears*) That was . . . I . . . horrible. We've
            been . . . police. Call the police.

BOB   Don't think so love. I had it coming to me.

PETULA   And Dougie. Unforgivable. Shouting at me.

DOUGIE   Come on Bubs. It was a siege situation. No tears eh?

PETULA   That's no excuse.

MARION   Bob. Bob. You're sure you're alright? I've got to
            go . . .

            (MARION *looks at the watch that isn't there.*)

            Damn. I've got to go to work. Need the car keys.

            (BOB *gives car keys to* MARION.)

BOB   Buzz me up when you get back. I'll meet you
            outside. Come up in the lift with you.

PETULA   I'm not moving. Could still be out there.

BOB   You'll be alright. He's got what he wanted. For
            now.

MARION   Petula. Dougie. I'll give you a lift to the station.

PETULA   I want a divorce.

MARION   Pen-Pen. Where's my sombrero?

PEN   Behind the sofa.

            (MARION *finds her sombrero.*)

MARION   Are you sure, Bob? I can phone in sick.

BOB   We need the money. Now more than ever.

MARION   Come on Petula. Help you with that. Cheer up.
            You're on holiday. Some of us live here.

            (MARION *helps* PETULA *out with her bags.*)

DOUGIE   I'd think about moving mate. Chummy boy next
           door isn't going to let you out of his sights.

           (BOB *walks onto balcony*.)

PEN   Have a nice play.

DOUGIE   Ha! Feel like I've just been in one. See you kiddo.

           (*Exit* DOUGIE. PEN *watches* BOB *for a while. He
           laughs*.)

PEN   What's so funny?

BOB   Just thinking. Lucky he didn't bring a bigger bag.
           Least we've still got the telly and something to
           sit on.

PEN   Dad. Dad. What's wrong?

BOB   Look at that. Beautiful. Isn't it beautiful? At
           night. Especially at night. That's the City, Pen-
           Pen. That's where it all starts. And this is where
           it all ends. Come out here sometimes. Dazzled by
           it. All that electricity. Burning away. Lighting up
           empty rooms. Eyes. Winking. Winking at you.
           Saying look at me. Look at how bloody bright we
           are. And behind each of those windows sits one
           of the types with his portable phone and his red
           braces and his striped shirt and his three hundred
           thou a year and his Porsche and his house and
           you think why me? Why am I over here? And why
           are they over there? Why? Who decided it should
           be like this? Who marked my card? Who saw me
           coming and pushed me through the door with No
           Hope written above it? And you stand here and
           you beat your chest for a bit and you swear and
           you yell and you stick two fingers up at the
           bastards and tell yourself they've robbed you and
           they're laughing in your face. And then it hits
           you. Maybe they're there. And I'm here. Because
           I haven't got what it takes. Can't cut the
           mustard. Can't hack it. Because I'm just not good
           enough.

(PEN *crosses to* BOB.)

PEN   Don't say that Dad. It's not true.

BOB   No?

          (BOB *grabs* PEN *and they hug.*)

BOB   Come here. Come here, kid. I love you Pen-Pen.
          Probably don't believe me. But I do. I'm sorry.
          You go, kid. Get out while you can. I don't blame
          you.

PEN   No.

BOB   What?

PEN   I don't want to go.

BOB   But I thought you . . .

PEN   No point in going if I haven't got somewhere to
          come back to. I'm going to stick around for a bit.

BOB   Pen-Pen Pen-Pen but what . . . how are . . .

PEN   Start all over again Dad, eh? Keep fighting, yeah?

BOB   Don't follow my example.

PEN   Not your way Dad. Don't have to belt someone to
          fight them. Come on. Let's clear up for Mum.

          (PEN *and* BOB *come inside.* BOB *clears away
          plates and cups.* PEN *crosses to heating grill.*)

BOB   Start again. You're right. If we have to move we
          have to move but . . . no. New beginning, eh Pen?

PEN   Don't think I would have liked Australia anyway.

BOB   Why not?

PEN   Never gone much for Jason Donovan.

BOB   I'll make your Mum some supper. Nice hot baked
          bean stew for when she gets in.

PEN   They're at it again. I can see one.

BOB   Here Pen. The shoe. Quick.

PEN   No. No, hang on.

           (PEN *lifts something from the heating grill in her
           cupped hands.*)

PEN   No Dad. We'll do it my way.

           (PEN *walks onto balcony.*)

PEN   I'm fed up with the dirt and the scum. There's
           only one thing to do. Throw it back.

           (PEN *throws cockroach out over balcony.
           Midaction — Blackout.*)